THE HUNGRY
OCEAN

LINDA GREENLAW

The Hungry Ocean

A SWORDBOAT CAPTAIN'S JOURNEY

COMPASS PRESS

AN IMPRINT OF WHEELER PUBLISHING, INC.

Published in Large Print by arrangement with Hyperion in the United States and Canada.

Compass Press Large Print book series;
an imprint of Wheeler Publishing Inc., USA

Set in 16 pt Plantin.

Map by Paul J. Pugliese

Library of Congress Cataloging-in-Publication Data

Greenlaw, Linda.
 The hungry ocean: a swordboat captain's journey / Linda Greenlaw.
    p. (large print) cm.(Compass Press large print book series)
   ISBN 1-56895-792-0 (hardcover)
   1. Greenlaw, Linda, 1960–. 2. Swordfish fishing—Grand Banks of
Newfoundland—Anecdotes. 3. Large type books.
I. Title. II. Series
[SH691.S8 G689 1999]
639.2/778b21

                                                              CIP

This book is dedicated to the men least likely to abandon a sinking ship:

Robert H. Brown

W. Alden Leeman

James S. Greenlaw

When I have seen the hungry ocean gain
Advantage on the kingdom of the shore,
And the firm soil win of the watery main,
Increasing store with loss, and loss with store.
                    —SHAKESPEARE, SONNET 64

CONTENTS

PREFACE

I have been fishing commercially for seventeen years, and up until the summer of 1997, nobody cared. With the publication of Sebastian Junger's *The Perfect Storm* came attention and opportunity. In general, people are intrigued with my life as the captain of the *Hannah Boden*, sister ship to the *Andrea Gail*, as portrayed in Junger's book, and their interest often results in questions about the day-to-day details of a typical month-long swordfishing trip to the Grand Banks of Newfoundland. Although the thrill of fishing is in the catching of fish, the greatest challenges any captain faces are often keeping the crew focused, making sure the vessel remains mechanically sound, and returning safely to port. To be considered a successful Grand Banks fisherman, a captain must manage three things: the boat, the crew, and the fish. Junger's portrayal of me as not just the only woman swordboat captain, but "one of the best captains, period, on the entire East Coast" has afforded me the opportunity to answer frequently asked questions and tell my own story.

Not to take away from the memories of the six men who were lost at sea with the *Andrea Gail,* or the multitudes of fishermen who have perished in storms that were less than perfect, but as Junger amply noted, fishing is just plain dangerous work, and tragedy on the ocean is often unrelated to weather. My personal story is not a tragic one. In *The Hungry Ocean,* I tell the true story of a real, and typical, swordfishing trip, from leaving the dock to returning. The action of the trip, along with stories from other trips, is interrupted for the necessary technical detail and description, and occasionally for the unnecessary personal observations and philosophies of the author, which might not interest all readers but are included because it is my book. Some of the interruptions come in short chapters between the bigger ones. I call these asides "mug-ups"—that's the term fishermen use to describe the very occasional coffee breaks we take in the middle of a day's or night's work.

Of the hundreds of fishing trips I have made, I chose this particular trip to write about mostly because of the crew. Five hardworking and interesting individuals, these men represent the typical offshore group; alone, each of these characters is worthy of his own book. In most instances I have used real names of people and boats, but a few composites and name changes were necessary for the protection of privacy. Dates, positions, weather conditions, and numbers of fish caught are all from actual logbooks. Using both my personal journals and the *Hannah Boden*'s Pelagic Longline Fishery Logbook, supplied by the United States Department of Commerce, I have been able to piece together the trip's technical information with accuracy.

Before I started this book the thought of time away from fishing, and a possible new career as an author, was strangely appealing. My life, exciting and dangerous, would take on some degree of normalcy, perhaps even become mundane. The often-heard complaints from some nine-to-fivers of repetition and boredom seemed attractive to me when I first considered writing a book. One year later, with my work on *The Hungry Ocean* nearly completed, I wonder daily if the opportunity to write this book has been a blessing or a curse. Writing has proven to be hard work, often painful. I can honestly say that I would rather be fishing.

1

TURNING THE
BOAT AROUND

It was very early in the morning, very late in
the month of August. The *Hannah Boden*
chafed against the pilings at Gloucester Marine
Railways, at her usual berth between trips. I
enjoyed a deep and restful sleep in my bunk
onboard, the type of sleep that nonfishermen
get most nights and fishermen get only when
all lines are made fast to the dock. I slept, and
it seemed all of Gloucester slept. All of
Gloucester, that is, except Bob Brown. The
stillness of the harbor was broken by the
ringing of my cellular phone. I was able to incor-
porate the high-pitched jingling into my dream
for the first fifteen or twenty rings. But I was
familiar with Bob's persistence and knew he
was not about to hang up; I had to get up and
answer the phone. I pulled a pair of sweatpants
up over my nightshirt and opened the door
between my quarters and the boat's wheelhouse.
As the phone rang on, I squinted at the clock.

"Oh, for Christ's sake, Bob, four-thirty..." I grabbed the receiver and said "Hi, Bob" as pleasantly as I could.

"Good morning, Linda. How did you know it was me?" The voice, sharp and clear on the other end, was wide-awake.

"Woman's intuition."

"I hope I didn't wake you," he lied.

"Oh, no, I've been up for hours," I said, trying to use sarcasm to mask my irritation.

"Well," he continued, "today is sailing day, and I thought you might like some breakfast before the boys show up. I'll pick you up in thirty minutes."

I hung up and finished the conversation to myself. "Luckily for you, Bob Brown, the one and only thing in this universe that I will sacrifice sleep for is food."

I nearly fell asleep in the shower. As the hot water pounded the back of my neck I thought about my boss. Although Bob Brown had proven himself a difficult man, I'd liked him upon meeting him, and my feelings hadn't changed over the years. I often found myself defending him to the five men who comprised my crew, whose attitude toward Bob was made up of equal parts of respect and repugnance. When somebody told me early on that I was working for the most hated man from Puerto Rico to Newfoundland, I laughed. But time had proven this to be true. No matter where I went, I would meet someone who knew Bob or had heard about him, and who would inevitably ask, "How can you work

2

for that asshole?" My answer seldom varied: "He's not so bad. He's got the nicest boat in the fleet, the best equipment money can buy, and he treats me well."

Bob was a smart man and couldn't possibly have been totally oblivious to the general fishing community's dislike of him, although it appeared that he was. He managed to take everything in stride, as if this ill will simply went with the territory; he was far too busy to waste time acknowledging any criticism. There will always be people who question extreme success, and with everything Bob touched turning to gold, there was a lot of talk. Some criticisms had merit, some were cheap shots born of jealousy. Bob had obviously stepped on a few fingers on his way to the top, and although some said that he had also picked a few pockets, I had never seen any dishonesty in my experience with him. He was an amazingly clever person; his competence covered a wide range. Among other things, Bob flew his own plane and was a top-notch mechanical and electrical troubleshooter. As for determination—he would take a boat to Mars if he thought there might be a fish to be caught there. Today the name Bob Brown is recognized by the millions of readers of *The Perfect Storm* as the owner of the *Andrea Gail*.

My only real problem with Bob, I thought as I dried my hair with a towel, was that he demanded so much of people. He naively expected everyone he came into contact with to think and act on his level. I worked hard to live up to Bob's expectations and usually fell short. Bob's approval was something I strove for, and seldom achieved, but it was one of the things that kept me going during my five years under his employ. As I tied my shoelaces, I concluded my thoughts on Bob Brown: Our relationship worked.

The tide was half and rising, making it an easy step from the rail of the boat up onto the dock, where Bob's truck was just easing to a stop. The man behind the wheel was of impressive stature. Bob was not tall, by any means, but what he lacked in height was more than compensated for in width of shoulders and girth of chest. His was a body built for physical work, low to the ground and rugged. As I climbed into the truck I made some smart-assed comment about the risk involved in riding with Bob Brown through the streets of Gloucester: "What if I'm hit with a bullet intended for you?"

Bob laughed, shaking his short and neatly combed, not quite to the salt-and-pepper stage, black hair. Stroking his clean-shaven chin with a hand that resembled a bear's paw, Bob thoughtfully offered, "Perhaps you would prefer to walk."

"No. I feel lucky this morning. You're buying, right?" I slammed the door and we made small talk as Bob drove to the restaurant.

Sitting across the table from Bob, I started

to get the first twinge of nervousness. It happened every trip, the day we were to leave the dock. I wondered what chore we had forgotten, what item I had neglected to put on my list, and how hard it would be to do without that particular item over the course of thirty days at sea. I pulled my checklist from my back pocket and went over it for what seemed to be the hundredth time since I'd brought the *Hannah Boden* back into Gloucester two days before. Preparing a boat for a month-long fishing trip involves so much work and such a high degree of organization that when the time comes to cast the lines off the dock, I have often breathed a sigh of relief, knowing that the most unpleasant part of the trip is over and the best is yet to come—the actual catching of fish, the reason most of us are in the business. Intense anxiety stood between that sigh of relief and myself this morning. There were still tasks to be completed after breakfast, before the lines could be thrown from the dock, indicating the official start of our September trip.

A waitress took our orders and filled our coffee cups. While we waited to be served, I fidgeted. I drummed the fingers of my left hand on the tabletop and bounced both legs up and down on the balls of my feet as I stared at the worn-out piece of paper in front of me. My mind raced through the events of the past forty-eight hours while the question lingered... What have I forgotten?

On August 26, my crew and I had landed

in Gloucester with the biggest trip of swordfish of my career, unloading over 56,000 pounds. The pride and excitement I felt over the previous trip did nothing to ease the tension and anxiety for the coming one. In fact, today I felt even greater pressure than usual. We would surely be expected to repeat in September what we had accomplished in August, and the first critical steps in that direction would be taken today. I had prepared for these trips so many times in the past that everything should have been more routine, less frantic. But so much was riding on the success of each trip during the short Grand Banks season that it was impossible to relax. I had heard of, and too many times lived through, difficulties caused by not fully preparing for a month at sea. The owner, the captain, and the crew all must pay strict attention to every detail that could affect the outcome of a trip. At sea you need to maximize your control over everything you can, to minimize the effects of those things you can't control, such as Mother Nature, who is known by all fishermen to be quite temperamental, and often a nuisance.

Bob Brown was the epitome of organization and a master of "turning the boat around," repairing, maintaining, and re-outfitting a boat between trips. Brown was known and admired for his unheard-of two-day turnarounds for Grand Banks trips. My head was spinning with the whirlwind of tasks that had been completed in the past forty-eight hours.

Bob Brown was the only boat owner I have worked for who, upon our homecoming from thirty days at sea, yelled to me from the dock before the first line was made fast, "When are you leaving again?"

Two days ago, when the last of the 527 swordfish, 118 bigeye tuna, and 7 mako sharks had been hoisted from their saltwater ice beds in the *Hannah Boden*'s fish hold and placed aboard trucks headed to Boston and New Bedford to be sold, we began the scrubbing and sanitizing of the fish hold. While the cleaning was being done, Tom Ring, my first mate and cook, headed to the grocery store to "grub up," shop for food for the six of us for the next thirty-day boat ride. Ringo had been in the business for nearly twenty years and was among the best crew members with whom I had ever had the pleasure of working. Not only is Ringo a first-rate deckhand and a good-natured shipmate, he's also an excellent cook, a key element in any successful and happy fishing operation.

Ringo has the amazing ability to shift gears, something that mediocre crewmen lack. Ringo's strength and endurance go well beyond what one might expect from a man of his size and build, which were deceptively average. Lacking excessive bulk, the muscles in Ringo's upper body were well defined by the years of physical work that he had chosen and loved. At some point in every trip, everyone reaches a stage of exhaustion unimaginable to anyone who has never quite been there. It is a state way beyond dead tired, a fatigue that goes all the way to the bitter end of each and every hair on your head. Just about the time I think the guys will start dropping on deck, Ringo musters some untapped resource within himself and goes into overdrive. Until hiring Ringo, I had always been the pacesetter, the prodder. (No self-respecting fisherman will allow himself to be outworked by a woman; it is a fact that brought the best out of my crew for years.) Now we all took pride in keeping up with Ringo.

Kenny and Carl, at twenty-two and nineteen respectively, the two youngest members of my crew, had climbed out of the fish hold with their scrub brushes just as a tractor-trailer truck was backing down the wharf. "All done! You could eat off the deck down there," said Kenny as he sat on the starboard rail and lit a cigarette. Pulling off his Boston Red Sox hat, Kenny exposed his bright orange hair, which matched his also naturally fiery temper. The other three men were kicking off their oil gear (foul weather or deck clothes consisting of rubberized bib overalls, hooded jackets, and knee-high rubber boots) when the screech of air brakes on the dock brought their attention to the tailgate of the truck, which had come to a stop just short of the edge of the wharf. The men looked at one another, then at the truck, and then at me.

Charlie, whose oil pants were now down

around his ankles, let out a long disgusted sigh. "Please tell me that truck is not full of bait." Exhaustion had dimmed his blue eyes' usual brightness, and the stubble on his cheeks concealed deep dimples. Even Charlie's posture begged for a break. "We're not putting the bait on tonight, are we?"

Before I could answer, the driver threw open the back door of the truck and we all stared at the mountain of boxes stacked clear to the ceiling and as far back into the body as we could see. "Fuck!" yelled Kenny, his red hair standing at attention. He flicked his cigarette into the harbor and paced back and forth across the deck while launching into a signature Kenny tirade. He barked loudly the pointed syllables of words heavy with his native Newfoundland accent. "Oh, for fuck's sake. Six o'fuckin'clock. Twenty-six days at sea, work your ass off, come in with a big trip, work your ass off unloading the fish, scrub the fuckin' fish hold. All I want to do is take these slimy fuckin' clothes off, jump in the shower and go up the street. Is that asking too much? I guess the fuck it is. We've been tied to this fuckin' dock for twelve hours and I haven't even set one foot on dry land yet. I just want to get off this fuckin' boat—"

"Well, now's your chance," I cut in. "Jump into the back of that truck and start handing that bait down here." Carl hopped up onto the dock to take his place as the second link in the human chain, while Peter, the tallest of the crew, stepped up onto the rail, becoming link number three. After one look at the long faces of my crew, a passerby would certainly have thought that they had just been sentenced to life in prison. Although it seemed unfair, Bob Brown had learned the hard way that he needed to get the crew to do everything humanly possible before handing them pay-checks and watching them disappear into the darkened doorways of the local barrooms. Kenny had recovered from his tantrum and was in the back of the truck; the others were pulling their oil gear back on. "Let's have a look at the stuff before we put it all aboard," I said, recalling preparations for a recent trip when I had refused 12,000 pounds of squid, sending it back to the cold-storage plant because of its poor quality.

Kenny jumped out of the truck with a 40-pound cardboard box of frozen bait and laid it on the rail of the boat, opening the top for my inspection. The bait was as gorgeous as any squid could be. Perfect in size, color, and condition, the squid had been laid in the box in a pattern similar to that of sardines in a can. The top layer of squid retained their tubular shape, not flattened or squished as some I had mistakenly accepted in the past. Each squid, about 10 inches from head to tail, was the color of a ripened eggplant, neither washed-out-looking nor freezer burned. The appearance of the bait triggered anticipation of what this squid might attract. I had learned through the years what now might sound obvious: the better the bait, the better the catch. Small swordfish and sharks are not nearly as finicky about what they eat as the larger fish. Markers, or swordfish over 100 pounds dressed weight (carcass weight minus head, fins, and guts), command a better price than pups (99 to 50 pounds), puppies (49 to 26 pounds), or rats (under 25 pounds). Better bait, better fish, better price, better paycheck. The buck starts here. Painfully, one 40-pound box at a time, with backs and biceps burning, six tons of frozen squid went into the *Hannah Boden*'s bait freezer.

The motions of Carl and Peter, two consecutive links of the chain, each handing boxes to the next in line, were like the working of two intermeshed gears of contrasting sizes turning within a machine. Each produced the same amount of output, but the input seemed vastly different. Carl's moves were quick, acutely angular, and sporadically powerful, while Peter worked with the graceful power and strength of long and smooth motions. Peter was fluid, and Carl solid. The looks in their eyes and set of their jaws also revealed opposite attitudes. Peter appeared content and relaxed enough to lie down and take a nap, while Carl was impatient, irritated; he was in a hurry to get the job done.

Just as the last box was pulled from the truck, a second truck backed down the wharf. Bob and Ringo appeared from inside the second truck's cab. The groceries were here: all fifty-odd boxes of them. Once the gro-

11

ceries were aboard, the men worked together to separate and store the "grub" in the refrigerator, freezer, and cupboards, and under the bench seats around the galley table. When the $3,500 of food was stowed to the cook's satisfaction, the men collected their paychecks from the previous trip and disappeared, not to return until eight o'clock this particular morning, still a few hours ahead as I sat over breakfast with Bob.

I dipped one last bite of fish cake into the egg yolk, shoved it into my mouth, and hoped this trip would not be long enough to use all of the 12,000 pounds of bait, and that the $3,500 of groceries would be more than enough to keep us satisfied until returning to port. My obsessing over the amount of supplies was interrupted by a fishy-smelling young man who appeared at the side of our table. "You're Linda, aren't you?" he asked.

"Yes, I am."

"I work for Peck on the *Hellenic Spirit*. Congratulations on your trip, I heard it was a slammer."

"Ha," Bob jumped in. "She would have had a real slammer if she had fished a few more nights."

I smiled and tried to ignore Bob's comment. "You haven't met my boss, the very pushy and never satisfied Bob Brown."

The two men shook hands, and as the fishy smell backed away from the table he added,

"I just wanted to say hello. I've never met a fisherwoman before. Good luck."

"Thanks. You too," I said, and shook my head at his use of the word *fisherwoman*. I hate the term, and can never understand why people think I would be offended to be called a *fisherman*. I have often been confused by terms such as "male nurse," wondering if that would be someone who cares for only male patients. *Fisherwoman* isn't even a word. It's not in the dictionary. A fisherman is defined as "one whose employment is to catch fish." That describes me to a tee. Generally, when the conversation reaches the point at which the person with whom I am speaking asks what I do for a living, I assume he or she has already determined that I am female, leaving *fisherman* appropriately descriptive of my occupation. *Fisherwoman* would at best be redundant.

The waitress came and cleared our plates from the table and refilled our coffee mugs yet again. Bob scowled at me with his sharp, black eyes and asked, "Do you really think I'm pushy?"

"Yes. Do you really think I should have stayed out longer last trip?"

"Yes. You had nearly six thousand pounds of fish your last day, and you headed for the barn. The *Hannah Boden* needs seventy-thousand-pound trips when the fish are there to be had. You should have stayed."

I gulped. Jesus, when was the last time anyone landed 70,000 pounds? "Well, I could have stayed. Should'a, would'a, could'a, but

I didn't. The moon was going down, and I didn't want to screw up this trip by missing some of the September moon."

"What if the weather turns sour or the water cools off early this year? You don't know that the fish will still be there this trip," Bob argued.

"They'll still be there. If we leave today, we'll be on the fishing grounds the day before the first quarter. We're gonna have another slammer."

Bob nodded. He had swordfished for years, and he believed in the importance of keeping trips in sync with the lunar cycle. Usually the most productive nights are two and three days either side of the full moon. Ideally, fishing should start the night of the first quarter of the moon and end on the last quarter. Steaming, traveling to and from the fishing grounds, and time at the dock should be during the darkest part of the lunar cycle, around the new moon. This is why Bob was adamant about quick turnarounds. Some captains favor fewer, longer trips, staying out forty-five, or even sixty, days at a time. My friend Charlie Johnson is one of these guys. Paying little attention to the number of days at sea, he always catches his share of fish, but has become known as "two-moon Charlie." I preferred to avoid seemingly endless voyages.

Staring at the cups on the table, I thought how nice it was that they just sat there with no one holding them to keep them from sliding onto the floor and smashing to bits. It seemed an insignificant thing to appreciate, yet it was something I would not see for another thirty days. I shifted my focus back to the list and once again concentrated on preparations. While the crew had taken two days for R and R, the boss and I had worked at maintenance to ready the *Hannah Boden* for another month at sea.

The *Hannah Boden* was immaculately maintained; Bob Brown saw to that. This 100-foot length of manicured steel, the width of a double-wide trailer, would be everything to the crew and myself for the next thirty days. She would be home to the six of us, our platform for work, our place of worship, our center for entertainment, our source of pride. The *Hannah Boden*, built like a well-endowed woman, inspires wolf whistles from those who truly appreciate fine marine architecture. Cosmetically, she is of clear complexion, with no rust blemishing her dark green hull or her bright white topsides. Bob Brown was a stickler for maintenance, which gave us all a sense of security when heading to sea on one of his vessels. I remember clearly the look of horror in Bob's eyes when he relayed a story of witnessing an employee of a shipyard painting the deck of a boat and "painting right over the top of a flounder!" This action, something that caused most of us to laugh, made Bob cringe, and he vowed to never employ this particular yard to service any of his vessels again. I was running the nicest boat in the fleet, and intended to help keep her that way.

Just twenty-four hours before, we pumped 10,000 gallons of diesel fuel aboard, filling the six tanks to their capacity, a total of nearly 20,000 gallons and enough for sixty days, twice the amount burned in a regular trip. We changed oil and filters on the main engine, a 3412 Caterpillar, the *Hannah Boden*'s source of propulsion. We serviced the pressurized air system that drives the engine's throttle and clutch controls, and cleaned the strainers on the suction lines of the electric pumps, all of which are powered by AC generated by one of the two 3304 Caterpillar engines onboard. We filled with distilled water the cells of the two 32-volt banks of batteries that supply the current for the DC systems onboard. All of the oil from a 55-gallon drum was pumped into the lube oil holding tank, and the dirty lube oil was pumped out of its holding tank. We charged the saltwater ice machine's compressor with Freon, pumped grease from a grease gun into an endless number of fittings located all over the boat, and ran errands to retrieve several odds and ends such as spare filters, lightbulbs, flashlight batteries, and duct tape.

The only thing that remained on my to-do list was stowing the new fishing gear. The gear had been ordered over the phone before we arrived in port and was now in the back of Bob's pickup truck. The gear, also called tackle, needed each trip is extensive; although longlining is a relatively simple fishery, tackle is a heavy expense, usually totaling close to $10,000 per trip.

Gear, fuel, bait, and miscellaneous items generally add up to a total of around $40,000 per trip. This cost is considered the operating expense and is subtracted from the gross profit before any money is divvied up into shares. So, roughly speaking, we needed to catch 10,000 pounds of swordfish to cover the expenses, and expenses must be covered before anyone would make a dime. All calculations are put on a piece of paper called a "settlement sheet"; the process of receiving pay is referred to as "settling up."

The principle of working for a share is something I have explained time and time again to prospective crew members, especially the green guys who have never fished commercially before. My explanation is usually part of a general warning meant to let them know what they are getting themselves into before they commit to a trip. If we don't catch fish, we don't get paid, period. There are no benefits, no salary, and no minimum wage. There exist no nine-to-five swordfishermen; in fact, twenty-hour days are the norm once we get the first hook wet. The game is never postponed due to darkness, and seldom delayed for weather. There are no weekends, no holidays, no personal or sick days. When the lines are cast from the dock, all time cards are considered punched "in," not to be punched "out" for over seven hundred hours— seven hundred hours of physical labor, in poor conditions, that you might not be paid for. In short, there is no labor union.

This is all spelled out quite clearly in the Sea Star Corporation's Employment Agreement, which all employees of the *Hannah Boden* are required to read and sign before embarking on their first trip. Included among the typical statements forbidding drugs, alcohol, and firearms onboard are an astonishing number of stipulations and contingencies that affect the size of paychecks, and a multitude of reasons for employment to be terminated with no compensation. I refer to the agreement as "Bob Brown's license to steal" and signed one many trips ago, trusting Bob to treat me fairly, which he has.

By the time Bob paid our breakfast tab, my nervous twinge had escalated to full-blown apprehension and near panic fueled by the knowledge that when we reached the Grand Banks five or six days from now we would be over 1,000 miles from the dock and any supplies I might have forgotten. Each step I took toward Bob's truck took me that much closer to the point of no return. Although satisfied that every item on my list had been checked off, there was always the chance that I had neglected to put something on the list, had overlooked some crucial detail. By the time we arrived back at the boat I was able to calm the butterflies in my stomach only by convincing myself that whatever I had forgotten, if anything, could not be very important or Bob would surely have noticed.

Stepping aboard the boat, my left foot reluctantly left the dock, not to return for at least thirty days. The clock was closing in on eight A.M.; the crew would be coming down the wharf any minute now. I looked optimistically up the dock. The panorama of the railways was chopped into sections like frames of film by the splintered pilings that had greeted and waved good-bye to so many boats in the past. I thought briefly how appropriate it was that I had stepped from the final frame of film already developed and into that which was yet to be exposed, a fresh start. I hoped that my crew would soon take the same step as easily as I had. As if reading my mind, Bob said, "I hope the men are on time."

"They'll be here." I feigned confidence.

"I hope they are sober and not too hung over."

"Don't count on it." I had been in the business of fishing for too long to expect, or even hope, that all five men might show up to work on time and sober. Although they were quite a rowdy bunch while ashore, I knew that my present crew was the best in the fleet. And regardless of their condition and the time they might appear this morning, these five were choirboys compared to some I had hired in the past. For instance, I can't imagine I will ever forget the group I enjoyed while running the *Gloria Dawn* out of Portland, Maine, and in particular a character called Uncle Patty.

2

MUG-UP

It was bitter cold in Portland, Maine. The
memory of that frosty December morning in
1987 sends chills up my spine that land on the
back of my neck and act as a reminder of the
worst decisions I have ever made. Parking
my truck in the lot, I headed down Hobson's
Wharf on foot. My crew of six men had been
working aboard the *Gloria Dawn* for about a
week at the dock, rigging her over for halibut
fishing. The *Gloria Dawn* was the first boat I
had captained, and I had been swordfishing
with her for the past several months. A 68-foot
fiberglass trawler, she was built at Desco
Marine in St. Augustine, Florida. The sticker
in the wheelhouse window proudly displayed
the manufacturer's motto: "The sun never sets
on Desco Marine." Unfortunately, quite the
opposite was true of the *Gloria Dawn*, whose
name sounded to me like a breakfast cereal.
Swordfishing had been a bust that season,
and we had dreams of bailing ourselves out
financially with a slammer trip of halibut.

The only tracks in the frost on the wooden planks of the dock were those I left of size-six Bean boots. The guys had not yet shown up to work for the day. I liked being the first one aboard in the morning, usually arriving at the dock early enough to allow time to complete the engine room chores before beginning work on deck. The tide was quite low, and I was wishing I had worn a pair of gloves as I climbed down the icy steel ladder on the side of the wharf. Stepping from the last rung across to the starboard gunwale, I hopped down onto the deck, disturbing the dusting of fresh snow. I blew into my cupped hands and scurried through the door and into the warmth of the fo'c'sle.

I stood directly in front of the small electric heater and cursed the winter. Talking to, and answering, oneself aloud is the result of too much time spent offshore, and is a habit that does not go away once formed. "Holy shit! It's cold! Ha, it's only December, and you're tied to the dock. How will you feel offshore in February? Miserable, that's how you'll feel, miserable...." I opened the engine room door and made my way down the ladder, the volume of the diesel-powered generator increasing with my descent. By the time the bottom rung was reached, the drone was loud enough to drown out my complaints, so I terminated the monologue and started my daily routine.

I measured the level of fuel in both starboard and port tanks, then checked the glass on the expansion tank above the main engine for the coolant level. Next, I pulled the dipstick from the main engine and examined it, finding oil up to the "full" mark. Replacing the dipstick, I hit the starter button and prayed. After some grinding and a few coughs, the main engine reluctantly started, and I allowed it to run while I serviced the generator. Supplying electricity for the appliances, heat, pumps, and lights, the generator is the boat's power plant.

The stuffing box around the shaft of the *Gloria Dawn* had a perpetual leak that no amount of packing could cure. At first it was disconcerting to witness the water flowing freely from around the shaft and into the bilge, but the last few months had hardened me to our varying states of sinking. Turning open a valve, I switched on an electric pump and discharged overboard the water from the bilge below me, filling Portland Harbor back to its proper level. I glanced at the bubble-filled sight glass on the Freon line of the bait freezer's compressor, was satisfied that things were in their usual state of disrepair, and made my way back topside.

The wheelhouse clock read six-thirty A.M. "They probably won't show for another half hour, so I might as well go up the street for a coffee," I sputtered to myself, and headed back outside, zipping my coat to the top of the collar. From the rail of the boat, I reached across to the steel ladder with one hand. I grasped a frosty rung and stepped across with one foot. As I pulled myself to the dock, something below me caught my eye, something in the water between the boat and the wharf. I climbed back aboard the boat and looked down into the water. There was no mistaking it: A human body was suspended in an upright position between me and the ocean floor, only the crown of the head breaking the frigid surface. "Oh, Jesus!" I looked up the dock toward the parking lot, willing one of my crew to appear, but the lot remained as still as the body below me.

I bent over the starboard gunwale and stretched my right arm down toward the head, my fingertips just inches from the brown matted hair. Scooching my belly across the rail so that only the toes of my boots remained in contact with the deck, I was able to grab a tuft of hair. With my left hand clutching the edge of the gunwale, I wiggled backward until most of my lower half was aboard the boat again; the top of the head was now bobbing slightly closer to the hull. Taking a deep breath, I pulled on the fistful of hair until a ghostly white face emerged just an arm's length from my own. The head's lips and eyes were nearly identical shades of blue. My heart was beating like a drum, and I felt breakfast rising in my throat. I swallowed and considered releasing my grip, allowing this dead man to drift away. Just then, his mouth dropped open and he spoke. "Wildman's dead, Captain."

"Hey, you're alive!"

"No, I'm dead."

"No, you're not. Not yet. Lift an arm up here and I'll try to pull you out."

"I can't. I'm dead." With this he closed his eyes and exhaled a long, slow breath that smelled about 100 proof.

"Yeah, right, you're dead. Dead drunk." At this point I didn't know whether he had died, passed out, or simply didn't feel like arguing with me, but it was clear that he was unable to help save himself. If he was still alive, I thought he surely would not last long in the freezing water. I pulled up on the hair and was able to reach his collar with my left hand. Yanking on the collar, I released my grip on his hair and grabbed his coat between the shoulders with my right hand, straining every muscle in my body against the dead weight of the man and his sea-soaked clothes. Pulling with my right hand again, I could reach the belt around his waist with my left. With my hands grasping his coat and belt, I gave one big heave and he flopped like a dead fish onto the fiberglass deck, where he lay crumpled up on his side in the puddle that had formed around him. As I stood over him catching my breath, two shadows joined mine on the deck.

I turned toward the dock to see my first mate and Timmy, another member of my crew. The mate was Portland Irish and had been working with me for a while; he was responsible for the hiring of the rest of the crew. As a result, I had a boatload of Portland Irish. They were heavy drinkers, hard workers, and loyal shipmates. The mate himself was a natural.

Everything he did aboard the *Gloria Dawn* he did with perfection and ease. He was a tough man with a mean streak that brought the best out of the worst of men, which pretty well describes the rest of the crew.

The two men hopped aboard. Timmy was the first to speak. "What happened to Uncle Patty?" he asked, rolling the body onto its back.

"He's your uncle?" I asked.

"Yeah, my dad's brother."

"I found him in the water. I think we should call an ambulance. I don't know how long he was overboard."

Suddenly, Uncle Patty moaned and his eyes popped open. "She pulled my hair," he said quite matter-of-factly.

The mate chuckled. "I told you not to fuck with her. What did she do? Throw you overboard?" He grabbed Patty by the shoulders and jerked him to his feet. Timmy helped steady his uncle. "Let's hold off on the ambulance, Linda. We'll get him into some dry clothes and he'll be fine."

"He scared the shit out of me. I thought he was dead," I called after them as they disappeared through the door leading to the crew's quarters.

Before the door banged closed, I heard Timmy's reply, "Good thing he's drunk. He'd have frozen solid if not for the booze in his blood. Probably the only thing that saved him." I swallowed breakfast yet again.

Figuring that the mate and Timmy had their hands full drying Uncle Patty off and out,

I decided to go for that cup of coffee. "Never a dull moment," I sighed, and climbed behind the wheel of my truck. Driving down Commercial Street, I replayed the morning's events. The image of the white face and blue lips was stuck in my mind's eye, and my stomach churned as I turned left into the Old Port section. I whispered, as if ashamed of my thoughts, "Old Uncle Patty gives me the creeps. If I never see him again it will be too soon." In an attempt to distract myself, I tuned the truck's radio to WPOR. I thought perhaps a little country music might stomp the haunting blue eyes from my brain, and I concentrated on the beat as I bumped along the narrow cobblestone street.

Suddenly, a yellow Volkswagen backed out into the street ahead of me. I hit the brakes and skidded to a stop, missing the lemon-colored fender by inches. The gentleman at the wheel looked a little embarrassed, flashed a wave, and mouthed "Sorry." I waved back, said "No problem," and smiled with the realization that it would be just twenty-four hours before I would be heading to sea, and it might be thirty days before I would bump into anybody but my crew. Proximity gains magnitude on the ocean. At sea, an approaching target at a distance of 6 miles on the radar screen, moving at a speed of only 10 knots, represents a possible threat to safety and is closely watched to ensure clear passage. Here in the city, vehicles ride on one another's bumpers at breakneck speeds and no one gives it a second thought. The Volkswagen skittered off ahead of me, dragging with it from my head all remaining thoughts of Uncle Patty. Deciding to forgo the coffee, I turned back toward the boat.

Five of the six members of my crew were now on the deck of the *Gloria Dawn* and were busy putting together tubtrawls. Tubtrawls are a type of gear used to catch halibut and other fish that feed on the ocean floor. As I climbed down onto the boat, I called, "Hi, guys. It looks like we'll be throwing the lines off the dock tomorrow. We'll get fuel and bait today, and groceries first thing in the morning." Then I asked the mate what he'd done with Uncle Patty.

The mate answered without looking up from his pile of hooks. "We changed him into some dry clothes and put him into his bunk. He's sleeping it off."

"*His* bunk?"

"Yup. The guy who was going to cook this trip has to spend a little time in jail. I hired Patty to take his place." The mate looked as if he were bracing himself for the wrath he deserved and expected to get.

I knew it would not be wise to have a screaming tantrum aimed at my best man in the presence of the rest of the crew, so I took a deep breath and thought for a minute. "How old is Uncle Patty?" I asked.

"Oh, I guess he's around forty-three," the mate answered, visibly pleased that I had not come unglued.

"He looks eighty-three to me," I snapped.

"Well, you caught him on a bad day. So, can he make the trip or not?"

I shrugged my shoulders and walked toward the wheelhouse door, shaking my head. "Jesus Christ! I'm taking Uncle Patty fishing."

Perhaps the worst of many bad decisions... I'll write more about Uncle Patty and the *Gloria Dawn* in chapter eleven. But now back to the *Hannah Boden*.

3

SECOND THOUGHTS

Although hardened from past experiences with crew, I clung to a wispy shred of optimism, silently hoping, but certainly not expecting, that my men might show up on time and in less-than-impaired states. Lack of crew had held boats to the dock on sailing day before. Many men gave in to the second thoughts that we all shared, and no-shows were not uncommon.

Perhaps it is alcohol that gives men license to back out at the last minute, some coming back to the dock to explain, others not showing up at all, saying nothing to anyone. A certain quantity of alcohol, once consumed, can surely dull the senses of responsibility and obligation, allowing men to go with their gut feelings, quitting without notice, refusing to sail. Some call it cowardly, others think it plain smart. We are all aware of the stories of seagoing prophets, those men who jumped ship just prior to setting sail aboard a boat that eventually met with disaster, giving credit to some ominous feeling that overwhelmed them, forcing them back to the barroom.

Praying that none of my five men would experience a mystical revelation before we could travel beyond a distance at which they might be tempted to jump and swim back to the beach, I left Bob on deck to tinker with the controls for the ice machine and wait for the crew while I went below to check the oil in the main engine. Finding the oil up to the "full" mark, I replaced the dipstick and climbed two sets of steel stairs to the wheelhouse, where I started the main engine with the push of a button. The engine started easily and idled smoothly. Next, I walked around the *Hannah Boden*'s spacious bridge, turning on some of the numerous pieces of electronic equipment to allow them to warm up. I switched the two radars into the standby position, turned on the GPS, the video plotter, two lorans, two single-side-band (SSB) radios, and flipped the VHF radio to channel 16. Most of the other electronics would not be needed until later, so I left them turned off and returned to the deck.

I stepped out into the sunshine just as Peter and Charlie were climbing out of a taxicab with their seabags—duffels filled with fishing clothes, reading material, cigarettes, toothpaste, deodorant, and other sundries. These two crew members were as close to total opposites in physical appearance as any two humans could possibly be. Peter, a tall and robust black man with a serious demeanor, is a native of Grenada. His close-cropped hair and sideburns appeared to have just met with a barber. Charlie is a paler-than-pale, class clown type of guy from Massachusetts whose disheveled head came up to the middle of Peter's chest. Charlie looked a bit rough this morning, but both men were smiling as they called out hello and disappeared into the fo'c'sle to stow their gear. Well, two down, three to go, I thought. Charlie and Peter had obviously overcome any misgivings or second thoughts they might have had this morning; very few men turn and run once their bags are aboard.

Looking up toward the head of the dock, I could now see the remaining three fifths of the gang heading in my general direction, seabags slung over shoulders. Their strides, far from purposeful, brought them slowly and reluctantly closer. There was no sign of a bounce in Carl's youthful step this morning, and he straggled behind the other two. Ringo and

Kenny stopped, allowing Carl to catch up. As the three men stood talking, it appeared they were teetering on the brink of a decision. I had seen, heard, and been involved in this discussion before. Men who had, for the last forty-eight hours, absorbed all the booze they could hold were now deciding whether to go back to the bar and continue into drunken oblivion or step aboard the boat to practice temperance for the next month. Kenny pulled a pack of Marlboros from his shirt pocket, stuck a cigarette in his mouth, and then offered the pack to Ringo and Carl. Ringo helped himself to one. Carl shook his head no, his complexion showing a hint of green. This accomplished, they resumed their trek toward the boat, Carl falling behind once again. The tide was nearly high; it was eight A.M. sharp.

Ringo stepped aboard, bringing with him the smells of the barroom. The scents of stale beer and cigarettes clung to his jeans and oxford-cloth shirt and were trapped in his thick mop of blondish hair. "Hi, Bob. Good morning, Linda. What a beautiful morning to go fishing!" His voice clear and words concise, Ringo neither sounded nor appeared intoxicated, although he surely was. Kenny was right behind him; as he greeted us, I couldn't help but notice a number of lumps on his forehead, which looked bruised and sore.

"What happened to you?" I asked, staring at his battered forehead.

"I got caught in a rum squall."

"What hit you? Bacardi bottles?"

31

"No," replied Kenny. "Clay pigeons."

My interrogation of Kenny was interrupted by the sound of retching. Carl, who hadn't quite made it to the boat, was leaning into a wooden piling up near the bow and puking into the harbor. He heaved a while longer, then stood up straight and wiped his mouth with the front of his shirt.

I turned to Ringo. "Where was he drinking last night?"

"Ask me no questions, I'll tell you no lies...." Ringo's answer was exactly the one I expected. The crew always sticks together, which is as it should be. I had no interest in going to sea with a bunch of tattletales and mama's boys. However, at the age of nineteen, Carl was well under the legal drinking age of twenty-one.

"You do know that Carl isn't old enough to drink, don't you?" I asked.

"Linda, a man doesn't need to look at his birth certificate to know whether he's thirsty or not." Another typical Ringoism.

"But he's just a kid, not a man."

"Well, you treat him like a man aboard here," Ringo reasoned. "He works like a man and gets paid like a man. Why shouldn't he drink like a man?"

"Perhaps you should add 'pukes like a man' to his many attributes," Bob remarked, nodding his head toward the dock, where Carl was doubled over and spewing into the ocean again. I couldn't help but laugh with the others, and hoped that maybe Carl had learned his lesson. Things could certainly be worse. Regardless of their condition, everyone was assembled and more or less ready to go fishing. If Bob and I could keep them from entertaining their second thoughts for just a few more minutes, the five of them would be mine for the duration of the trip. Until the ill effects of alcohol wore off, they would feel like indentured slaves, and I would surely be accused of shanghaiing them before everyone was totally sober and free of hangovers.

I shouted up the dock to Carl to start handing the boxes of tackle from the back of Bob's truck down to the guys on deck. Charlie joined Carl on the dock end of the job, and within minutes the back of the truck was empty and the boxes were on deck, where we opened them one at a time, checking the contents off my gear order list. This trip's order consisted of:

1. Six cases of 300-pound-test monofilament fishing line (leader material)

2. Three 1-mile coils of 700-pound-test monofilament line (main line)

3. Three thousand 7698B Mustad hooks

4. Eight boxes of 1,000 D crimps (D refers to the size of the crimp or "sleeve" and is the size appropriate for 300-pound-test mono)

5. Two hundred snaps with swivels (snaps are a type of metal clothespin used to attach hooks to the mainline)

6. Two 12-inch bastard files (used to sharpen hooks)

7. Six slime knives (knives with curved blades, used to scrape the inside of a swordfish's body cavity when cleaning, or dressing)

8. Six 6-inch rippers (all-purpose knives)

9. Twelve meat saw blades (used for severing fins and heads from fish)

10. Four wire brushes (used to clean bits of blood from the spines of fish to avoid premature spoiling of meat)

11. Eight thousand chemical lightsticks: 2,000 white, 2,000 blue, 2,000 green, 1,000 yellow, and 1,000 pink (these are used to attract bait and swordfish to fishing gear)

We had everything.

As we sorted the gear it was Charlie's turn to vomit, and he did so over the port rail. "Jesus, I wish you guys wouldn't drink so much," I said to no one in particular.

"Yeah, wish in one hand and shit in the other.

See which one fills up first," said Kenny Lumphead.

"You are disgusting!" I turned to Ringo, who seemed rather to enjoy Kenny's eloquence, and asked, "Do they make clay ostriches?"

The guys lugged the boxes of gear inside and up to the forepeak, which is a large storage area in the very bow of the boat. Bob was looking into the ice machine with a flashlight and making small adjustments to the saltwater feed line. I hoped he would hurry and finish before one or more of the men disappeared.

"Linda, can I run up to Dunkin' Donuts for a minute?" asked Ringo.

"No. We're going to leave as soon as Bob is done tuning the ice machine."

"I'll only be a minute," Ringo tried again.

"The last time you went for doughnuts, you came back with a twelve-pack of Budweiser."

"I had doughnuts, too!"

"Dough*nut*. You had one doughnut."

"Didn't I give it to you?"

"I'm not hungry, and you're not leaving this boat."

"God, I hate sobering up." Ringo joined the rest of the crew along the starboard rail, where he sat down and lit a cigarette in resignation, putting the final touch on a picture of a truly ragged-looking crew. I watched over Bob's shoulder as he continued his work on the ice machine. Saltwater ice is a necessity on a Grand Banks boat. Four degrees colder than freshwater ice, it helps to keep the fish from spoiling on the long trips. When handled properly, the meat of a fish three weeks dead is just as nice as that of fish fresh off the deck.

As Bob watched the ice, I reached into my right-hand pants pocket for my Chap Stick. It wasn't there. I frantically searched my other pockets, coming up empty. My lips, which are very sensitive to sun, wind, and salt, would be chapped, cracked, and bleeding the entire month without a Chap Stick.

"Hey, Bob, I need to run to the store for a Chap Stick."

"Oh, no. You're not leaving this boat," he said. "The machine is all set. I'll throw the lines."

"Bob, I can't go a month without Chap Stick. My lips will never be the same," I pleaded.

"Here, take mine." He handed me a used Chap Stick from his pocket and quickly climbed onto the dock, where he bent over and grabbed the first springline. I understood Bob's refusal to let me stray from the boat, as I knew he had seen captains jump ship at the very last minute, leaving him with a bunch of drunken crew members who were quite anxious to follow their captain's lead.

Someone from the starboard rail wondered out loud, "What would he have done if she said she needed Tampax?" I shook my head and looked at the Chap Stick in disbelief. It was so old it was in a metal tube, the kind that had been superseded by plastic as far back as I could remember. This must be some kind of family heirloom, I thought, and vowed to not lose it or send it through the clothes washer and dryer, as I had done with so many before.

"Okay, let's go," I said to the guys, and climbed the stairs to the bridge. This was it; there was no turning back now. The men loosened the dock lines from the cleats, giving Bob enough slack to lift the eyes of the four lines up over the tops of the dock's pilings. The crew pulled the freed lines aboard the boat and coiled them neatly as I maneuvered the *Hannah Boden* slowly and carefully away from the dock.

Bob waved from the dock. "See you, fellas. Good luck, girl."

As the stern of the boat cleared the end of the dock, I turned the helm hard to port and headed for the red-and-green mid-channel marker. I breathed that long-awaited sigh of relief: "Too far for anyone to jump." Leaving the buoy to port, I steered out of Gloucester's inner harbor. As we glided by Ten Pound Island, Kenny appeared at the back door of the wheelhouse and asked, "Shall I lower the outriggers now?"

"Yes, please. We'll leave the birds up until we need them. Thanks."

The boat creaked and groaned as Kenny eased the outriggers, two giant steel arms whose purpose is to slow the motion of the boat in rolling or rough seas, from their upright position down to almost horizontal. The 200-pound steel stabilizers, called "birds," that hang by chain at the ends of the outriggers, are designed to dive or swim below the surface of the water, their tendency to dig in, adding resistance to the boat's roll. The birds also add slight resistance to the boat's forward motion as they are dragged through the water, reducing our speed by 1 knot. In fair weather the birds are left hanging in the air; they are lowered into the water hydraulically only when needed. The starboard bird remains hanging on the end of the outrigger every day while "hauling back," retrieving the fishing gear, regardless of weather conditions, as the gear is hauled aboard at the starboard side of the boat. If the starboard bird were in the water while hauling back, it would constantly become tangled in the mainline, and clearing it would consume precious time. At this point, we wouldn't have to worry about tangled gear for at least five days, until we reached our destination east of the Grand Banks of Newfoundland. Until such time, we would be "steaming," or traveling.

As the breakwater faded behind the boat I turned the autopilot on, keeping a heading slightly north of east, about 82 degrees true. I breathed a second sigh of relief: "Too far for anyone to swim." The sea was calm and visibility excellent, a great day to start the trip. I glanced out the back windows to the stern deck, where my five-man crew stood facing aft. I knew they would stand there until they saw Gloucester totally disappear, until the last speck of green sank into blue. I always did when I worked as a crew member. Things were different now. As captain, I had to force myself to look forward, over the bow, 1,000 miles to the east and five days into the future. Each trip it got a little more difficult to convince myself that the important things lay ahead and the things that remained behind would still be there when we returned. It was getting harder to dispel those second thoughts.

I hopped into the captain's chair and relaxed. The loran indicated that we were making a speed of 10.4 knots, which is about average for steaming in good weather with the birds up. The video plotter had the waypoints in it from our last trip out, the closest one to our present position being 25 miles south of Cape Sable, Nova Scotia, and 223 miles at 82 degrees from our present position. The plotter's screen, similar to that of a personal computer monitor, shows the boat's geographical position relative to waypoints introduced manually by the user. The boat appears on the screen as a blinking dot of about the same diameter as a pencil. I usually place a line on the screen running from the boat, or dot, to the next waypoint, that line representing our desired course. When the crew members stand watch, which they each do every night, they need only to keep the blinking dot on the course line to insure that the boat is heading in the proper direction, an ultra-slow-motion video game. Although my present crew were all competent seamen, and could navigate, the plotter is always a good safeguard against mistakes.

I stepped down from the chair and walked

over to the GPS, Global Positioning System. The GPS is a piece of electronics that uses information from satellites to calculate the boat's position in relation to latitude and longitude, and is highly accurate. The GPS may also be used to calculate range and bearing to a way-point. In other words, the GPS can tell me what distance and direction any certain point lays from me. I keyed our ultimate destination into the GPS's keyboard: 45 degrees 00 minutes north, and 45 degrees 00 minutes west. The GPS read: "Range: 1,102 nautical miles; Bearing: 82 degrees true." The screen also indicated that we were making a course of 85 degrees true, 3 degrees too many. I walked to the autopilot and turned the control knob a fraction of an inch counterclockwise to alter our course to port approximately 3 degrees.

Satisfied that we were now on course, I sat and relaxed again. I thought about the cellular phone mounted above the chart table, and how I should use it before we sailed beyond its range. The phone will usually work in its roam capacity all the way across the Gulf of Maine and partway up the coast of Nova Scotia before our course takes us too far from shore to connect with any land-based cellular phone facility. I had spoken with my folks on the way into Gloucester a few days before, telling them that I would try to get up to the island for a visit before leaving on another trip. Time was in short supply, and I never got farther than 3 miles from the *Hannah Boden*, never mind all the way up to Isle Au Haut,

Maine. It seemed the boat had been keeping me on a short leash this season, the choke collar type that reminds you instantly when you have wandered too far, too fast. There had simply been too much to do aboard the boat, too tight a schedule to allow for any time at home. Recently, I had become aware of the fact that I never called home from the dock, only from offshore, and usually when I was steaming out. I wondered what this said about my confidence in my ability to keep my nose to the grindstone. Surely my mother's voice on the phone telling me to come home for a few days would initiate second thoughts. The Grand Banks swordfishing season is a relatively short one, and I had to rely on making the bulk of my year's pay in four or five months.

In prior years we had extended the *Hannah Boden*'s sword season into November. However, since the loss of our sister ship, the *Andrea Gail*, in the Halloween gale of 1991, Bob Brown had insisted on ending our season by mid or early October to avoid the severe weather that normally occurs after that time. Through the years, on different boats engaged in a variety of different fisheries, I had managed to fish the Grand Banks every month of the calendar year, and had taken many a beating at the hands of Mother Nature because of it, the most brutal trouncings occurring in late fall. By the end of October this year, we would be rigging the boat and gear for offshore lobstering on Georges Bank or for swordfishing down in the Caribbean, either of which was preferable to fighting the winter weather at 45 degrees north and 45 degrees west.

I looked again at the cellular phone. "I guess I had better let someone know I've headed to sea again," I said out loud. I grabbed the receiver from its bracket and dialed my older sister, Rhonda, in Cundy's Harbor, Maine. Rhonda is the caretaker of the family and keeps tabs on us all.

"Hello."

"Hi, Rhon. What's up?"

"Hi, Lin! Not much. Where are you?" she asked.

"Aboard the boat, steaming out. We just left this morning. I thought I had better check in with you; it's been a while."

"Yeah, I talked to Mom last night. She said you had a great trip, congratulations!"

"Oh, thanks." I hesitated, afraid to ask. "Has anyone called for me?"

"No, Lin."

"Bill hasn't called?"

"Nope."

"Wayne?"

"Nope."

"Jesus...Larry Butler?"

"Larry hasn't called since last March."

"Well, you never told me that he called," I snapped.

"Yes, I did. You said if he called again to tell him you said hi."

"Well, did you?" I asked desperately.

"He hasn't called!"

"Oh. Well, what should I expect? Shit, he's

been married five times. He probably has that attention deficit disorder."

"Yes." Rhonda laughed loudly. "I guess they all do. Why don't you call them?"

"Didn't our mother teach us that it is improper for girls to call boys?" I reasoned.

"Hey. Great excuse! So...when did you start considering yourself a girl?"

And on that note we said our good-byes and good-lucks. I always give Rhonda's number to anyone who might want to get in touch with me, because she always knows my whereabouts and has a knack for getting rid of any unwanted attention and cultivating that which I might find desirable. For the past few months, it seemed, she hadn't had to do much of either. The *Hannah Boden* had consumed all of my time, leaving none for extracurricular activities such as boyfriends. I didn't have time to eat lunch, let alone work on a relationship.

I quickly forced from my head the depressing reality of no romantic attention for another thirty days, replacing it with, what else, another list. I grabbed my notebook and pen from the top of the chart table and plunked myself back into the chair. I leafed through the pages of old lists, watch bills, and many sheets where I had logged both fishing and personal information until I found a blank page on which I scribbled across the top: "Things to Do Before We Set Out the Gear." From my seat I could see the radar screen, the plotter, two lorans, and out the windows of the wheelhouse, forward and both sides. We were still on course, and there was nothing but ocean as far as the eye could see. This was one of the rare occasions when the ocean was totally still and the same color as the sky. Staring ahead, I couldn't distinguish where the ocean stopped and where the sky started; it was an eerie feeling. All the way around the boat, 360 degrees of nothing but blue. No waves, no other boats, no skyline, no land, nothing. Just a few hours out of Gloucester, and we might as well have been a ship in a bottle. A seascape absent of definition, the scene lacked the influence of some artistic flair. I searched my surroundings for a swooping gull or the flash of a fish on the surface, but found neither. Only solitude was portrayed on this canvas void of brush marks, or some might see loneliness. But loneliness is a state of mind, and although I was indeed alone, I would never be lonely.

Suddenly realizing that it had been a while since I had checked the engine room, I set my notebook aside and ran below two decks, putting on my headphonelike ear protectors as I went. Checking the engine room was quite simple and had to be done several times a day. At night, the guys check it every thirty minutes as part of their watch duties. I walked carefully around the machinery, examining sight glasses (clear tubes attached to the outside of tanks indicating the level of liquid within each tank), and temperature and pressure gauges. I looked around for fuel, oil, or water leaks, and checked the bilge. Happy that we were neither sinking nor on fire, I climbed up to the main deck level, closing the steel engine room door behind me. The galley was void of human activity. I opened the huge stainless steel door of the walk-in refrigerator, reached in, and grabbed a can of diet Pepsi—one of my necessities while at sea or ashore. Both the starboard and port stateroom doors were closed, and the lights were off down below in "the pit," indications that the crew were sleeping off their two days of leisure time. I climbed the stairs to the wheelhouse with my soda and a family-size bag of Lay's potato chips that had somehow found its way under one of my arms.

By the time I had formulated the new list in my head, I had devoured nearly the entire bag of chips, the remains of which I placed on the chart table. I would allow the crew to sleep today; the work would start tomorrow morning. Rather than constantly telling the crew what to do in preparing for the first set, I like to make a list of the things that need to be done, allowing them to decide among themselves the order and who will do each job. If the crew were green, there would be the need for me to baby-sit them, but these guys knew what needed to be done as well as I did, and I trusted them to all do their share. In fact, this gang would no doubt have the gear in order long before I found a piece of water on which to start fishing. I printed the list in block letters. Although I numbered the items, there was no order of priority. Everything had to be done, and each single item was just as important as every other. While the crew slept through the first leg of the trip, avoiding thoughts of sad good-byes and perhaps some welcome-homes they never received, I achieved the same by keeping busy with lists. Idle time made it too easy for the second thoughts to take over.

THINGS TO DO BEFORE WE SET OUT THE GEAR

1. Assemble and test beeper buoys

2. Sharpen all hooks

3. Adjust and test crimper

4. Make 2,400 leaders

5. Assemble and paint all bullet floats

6. Organize all floats in bundles of ten, and hang on port weather wall

7. Add 3 miles of mainline to spool

8. Put bands on lightsticks

9. Make slammer baits

10. Make ball-drops

It was a relatively short list. With the exception of making leaders and banding light-sticks, all the items could be completed in the first two days. The making of 2,400 leaders usually takes two men four days working twelve hours each day. I knew that Peter would oversee that tedious job and would probably make the bulk of the leaders himself.

A leader is an assembly of a metal snap, a length of 300-pound-test mono fishing line, and a hook. The snap and hook are fixed to opposite ends of the mono using a D crimp. The end of the mono is passed through the crimp, which is a half-inch-long sleeve of metal tubing with an oval-shaped opening twice the size of the mono's diameter. The same end of the mono is then passed through the eye of the hook; this is similar to threading a needle. Next, the end of the mono is pushed back through the crimp in the opposite direction, forming a loop of mono on which hangs the hook. The loop is tightened around the hook's eye by sliding the crimp and pulling the slack mono through it. This is done until the loop is closed around the eye. The crimp, filled with two strands of mono, is then placed into the jaws of the crimper, the tool used to squash the crimp down onto the mono to hold the assembly together. The crimper is adjusted so that the mono will not slip out of the crimp when strain is applied to the hook, but not so tightly that the mono will be damaged and break with the strain of a fish. Proper adjustment of the crimper is critical and is checked often. The snap is fixed to the other end of the mono in the same fashion. The metal clothespinlike snap is used to attach the leaders to the mainline when "setting out." Nine hundred leaders, snapped onto 40 miles of mainline, with floats between every two leaders and a beeper buoy every fifty floats, is considered one set aboard the *Hannah Boden*. With luck, fifteen sets would be enough for this trip. The length of leaders I fish on the Grand Banks is 7 fathoms. One fathom is equal to 6 feet. Hence, each leader would be 42 feet long. Peter had proven himself to be meticulous about keeping the gear up, and often stayed up all night by himself repairing and replacing leaders that had been damaged by sharks, fish, or snarls.

The other time-consuming and extremely boring job is placing rubber bands on each and every one of the 8,000 lightsticks. The only thing that makes this job at all bearable is the fact that it can be done while sitting at the galley table in the evenings watching a movie on the VCR. Rubber bands are used to attach the lightsticks to the leaders just prior to putting them in the water. Each leader gets a lightstick each night. A lightstick is a plastic tube 4 inches long that contains a chemical, and a smaller glass tube that is filled with some other chemical. When the plastic tube is bent, the glass tube inside it breaks, releasing the chemical within it, allowing the two chemicals to mix. When the two mix, the reaction produces light. This light is believed to attract swordfish and/or bait fish, depending upon whose theory you want to listen to. While setting the gear, the crew places a lightstick on each of the 900 leaders, about 1 fathom up from the hook. One end of the stick has a small eye, or hole, through which the rubber band is passed, looped through itself, and drawn tight. The sticks are banded prior to making the first set, as this is done most easily without gloves on and can't be done quickly enough to keep up with the speed at which the leaders must go overboard.

The only part I would personally take in readying the gear for fishing is testing the beeper buoys and making slammer baits. Slammer baits are a secret weapon used to attract swordfish to my gear. I learned of slammer baits from my friend Larry Butler, who no longer fishes for sword. I believe that the use of slammers gives me an edge over those who don't use them, and it's always nice to have an edge, or at least to think you do. Slammer baits are made by cutting slices from tube-shaped Styrofoam pipe insulation and soaking the slices in cod-liver oil. The oily rings are then placed in Ziploc plastic bags, where they resemble giant slices of black olives.

When setting out at night, before baiting a hook, the baiter first attaches the lightstick to the leader, then passes the hook through the ring of the slammer bait, and only then puts the squid on the hook, allowing the slammer to float up and down between hook and light. Slammers are not used on each of the 900 leaders each night but are spaced evenly along the 40-mile longline, usually one per every 20 or so hooks. I've never been quite sure they work, but I know that they don't hurt. I have always maintained that even if the slammers do not attract fish, the cod-liver oil works to mask the scent of cigarettes that must surely be on the crew's gloves, and cigarettes and other human smells certainly can't be good. At times my crews have considered me somewhat of a fanatic, but I would consider myself foolish to travel into the middle of the North Atlantic Ocean in pursuit of swordfish and ignore any possible advantage.

I tossed the notebook onto the table and squirmed around in the chair, trying to get comfortable. Bob Brown had furnished the *Hannah Boden* with the most uncomfortable captain's chair I had ever set my behind in. It had a dark brown vinyl cover stretched over what felt like unpadded wood and steel, and was totally straight-backed to make it nearly impossible for the occupant to fall asleep, a cardinal sin while standing watch. I say "nearly impossible" remembering what had occurred on a previous trip. Every captain's worst nightmare is to have the man standing watch while the others sleep fall asleep himself. With nobody paying attention, any number of things can go wrong, all adding up to disaster. With the watchman fast asleep, the boat could collide with a ship or run aground; or maybe a fire would start in the engine room and go unnoticed until it blazed out of control, forcing captain and crew to abandon the boat for the life raft, quite possibly never having the chance to call "Mayday" on the radio. Would the raft inflate properly? Would it leak? How long would it be before someone got concerned enough to notify the Coast Guard? Would the Coast Guard know where to search? Would they find us? Would it be too late?

All these questions raced through my mind when I fired a man for sleeping on watch. We were on our way home with a boatload of fish, just forty-eight hours from the dock. It had been a tough trip. Bad weather had tormented us from the beginning, and we were all exhausted from the relentless spell of Mother Nature. I had made it perfectly clear to the crew that if they couldn't stay awake for their ninety-minute watches they were to wake me. I would gladly relieve them—no penalty, no shame.

I usually sleep lightly when at sea, keeping track of how often the engine room door slams shut, noting who is checking the engine room regularly and who is not. I hear every creak and groan and notice the change in the sound of the generator when a pump or compressor kicks on. My best friend, and first captain, Alden Leeman had warned me many times never to relax: "Don't ever let your guard down, because the one time you do, you'll be in trouble. The trip is not over until you tie the boat to the dock." Alden Leeman taught me everything I know about catching swordfish,

51

and his warnings about safety and good seamanship will be with me forever.

I don't know how long the man had been sleeping when I woke him with a sharp backhand across his face—too long, I guess. I am not normally a violent person, and am still amazed that it didn't bother me to strike this man in the face. It seemed right. He opened his eyes to see me standing over him; I was sweating and trying to catch my breath. "I'm sorry," he said nonchalantly. "I must have dozed off."

"You could have killed us, you fucking idiot!" I screamed. Although I hear colorful language all the time, I was uncomfortable using it myself, and the word *fucking* sounded foreign to my ears, the full pronunciation of the *-ing* a dead giveaway of my unfamiliarity.

"What happened?" he asked.

I told him. I told him so loudly, and in so much detail, that by the time I had finished with him the rest of the crew had come up to the wheelhouse to see what all the commotion was about. I explained to them all how I had been awakened by a voice on the VHF radio. First, the voice called "The boat two miles east of me," then "one mile east of me," then "one-half mile east of me," and finally "one-quarter mile east of me." When I realized the voice was sounding rather stressed, and no one was answering his calls, I hopped from my bunk to listen to the rest of what was sounding quite urgent. As I poked my head into the wheelhouse, I was immediately horrified.

52

The windows across the front of the house were filled with white lights. We were so close to the lighted object that I couldn't determine what it was, but thought for sure we were about to crash into it. I cranked the helm over hard to starboard, pushed the throttle up to full ahead, and said a silent prayer. I watched out the port window as the end of the outrigger just missed the other vessel. My heart was in my throat as I steamed away from the lights. As the distance grew between the lights and myself, two distinct targets appeared from the center of the radar. I looked again at the lights out the window: three white lights vertically stacked, a tugboat. One single light far behind the tugboat indicated a barge. Looking into the radar screen again, I found that I had managed to put a half mile between the *Hannah Boden* and the tug with barge in tow. If I had reacted differently, we would surely have smashed into the tug or the barge, or run over the cable between the two, any of which would have been disaster. My response was more of a gut reaction than anything else. If I had taken the time to form a plan to avoid collision, it would have been too late. I had made a lucky guess, a guess that stood between the completion of a successful month at sea and grave misfortune. Images of twisted steel and bodies in the water flashed through my head, and that's when I'd slapped the man awake. He had slept through the whole incident and was surely going to face the consequences. I told the man he would *never*

53

work with me again and chased everyone from the bridge, vowing that I would drive the last forty-eight hours myself, which I did, my anger keeping me wide awake.

I never felt any remorse for striking the sleeping man, nor did I have any second thoughts about firing him. The memory of the near miss stirred my anger still, and I continued to squirm in the uncomfortable chair. Some people can sleep anywhere, I thought, and Alden is right; I would have to be on my toes for the entire trip, until we tied the boat back to the dock. I had confidence in my crew, but I'd still sleep with my ears open.

The afternoon dwindled, and I watched the sun as it sank into the wake behind the boat, the blaze-orange ball making contact with the ocean's surface and disappearing into the cool depths. I could almost hear it sizzle. The last pink faded from the horizon, taking several degrees of air temperature with it. Ashore, the cooling in the evening is gradual, the heat of the sun slowly dissipating from the land that has been soaking it up all day. When the sun sets at sea, the drop in temperature is immediate, like turning a corner in the grocery store to enter the aisle of frozen pizzas—it's that sudden.

Tugging a sweatshirt on over my T-shirt, I stood facing the chart table. I jerked open the first drawer of the table and pulled out the top chart of a large stack. Closing the drawer with my hip, I spread the chart over the table. International Chart #404, a map published by the Canadian Hydrographic Service, covers a wide area of the North Atlantic Ocean and is titled "Gulf of Maine to Strait of Belle Isle." I found our position on the chart—42 degrees 50 minutes north and 68 degrees 28 minutes west, about 100 miles east of Gloucester and nearly due south of Isle Au Haut, Maine. I realized that this was as close as I would come to my home and family for another month, and was almost overwhelmed with sadness. The island, a pale-yellow-colored spot on the chart, was no bigger there than a grain of rice, yet it was powerful enough to cause me to reconsider so much. The feelings were intense, and because I had dealt with them before, I knew they were also temporary. I would allow this brief despair to run its course, my second thoughts being a natural part of each new beginning.

I walked over to the port side of the bridge, where I rested my arms on the windowsill and stared out dreaming in a northerly direction. My mind's eye, amazingly clear, turned the near darkness to bright sunshine. I saw a twelve-year-old girl on a beach holding a shell to her ear. She stared back at me, looking and listening for stories of the sea. But her concentration lacked intensity; her curiosity had been more than satisfied. She had seen and heard all that the sea had to show and tell, and appeared now only to be going through the motions. No longer seduced by intrigue, she was simply completing a routine. She was tired. Someone wiped a tear from an eye; I wasn't sure whether it was me or the child in my mind; it didn't matter.

I returned to the helm and sat back in the captain's chair. Why couldn't the girl just drop the shell? I wondered. It would be so easy to give in to the second thoughts. All I had to do was twist the knob on the autopilot, turning the boat around 180 degrees. I could be back in Gloucester first thing tomorrow morning and be home by lunchtime, leaving behind the pressures of maintaining the boat and crew, and catching fish, and pleasing the boss. My entire world was fishing. Where could I possibly go from here? And who cared? Who cared that I had sacrificed so much for my life of adventure? Who knew that I desperately wanted a husband, a house full of children, a boring job? How had I wound up here in the first place? Each time I sailed by the island, I felt the possibility of ever changing my life getting more remote, yet the longings grew stronger with each passage. The shell was the girl's identity, and she held it in a death grip.

4

MUG-UP

I am a woman. I am a fisherman. As I have said, I am not a fisherwoman, fisherlady, or fishergirl. If anything else, I am a thirty-seven-year-old tomboy. It is a word I have never outgrown. Neither abused nor neglected, I am the product of a blissful and unique childhood...a rare claim these days. Like all young children, I believed wholeheartedly in the words of my mother and father. It was only natural that I took seriously the assertions of my parents that I could do whatever I liked with my life, become anything I wanted. Although the advice was well intentioned, my parents never dreamed that it might come back to haunt them when I decided that what I liked, and wanted to become, was a fisherman.

I woke up one morning, at the age of twelve, to the smell of low tide. The scent of seaweed and tidal pools crept through my open bedroom window and tiptoed around the room, not overpowering, but arousing interest. Usually awakening to the faint smell of pine and the rush of wind in the trees, that day I was intrigued with the thick, musty odor of sun-baked salt and mussel-covered rocks. My ears strained to pick up the slight sloshing of the tide as it swept in and out around the low-water-mark rocks and ledges. It seemed strange that having been surrounded by the ocean my entire life, this was the first time I noticed the screeching of the gulls and the drone of a diesel-powered lobster boat nearby. I approached my bedroom window and, leaning on the sill, looked out to sea. The surface of the water sparkled, every ripple reflecting the color of the sun like millions of golden sequins. Dark and shaded, my usual playground of the woods behind our house never knew this type of brilliance.

The woods were comfortable. I knew every gnarled root and fragrant bayberry bush like the back of my own hand, and although I loved them, their total familiarity left me with no new challenges. Most of the fun had gone out of building forts and stalking squirrels with slingshots. There was something mysterious about the sea, something alluring. This day I would leave my slingshot and Swiss army knife on the back porch and, rather than head for the deep woods, I would wander down to the shore in Robinson Cove.

From the rocky beach beside my grandfather's dock I could see all the way across Penobscot Bay to the island of Vinalhaven.

Looking to the south, I could see Brimstone, a small lump of an island, and Saddleback Ledge, a stark rock with the lone structure of a lighthouse tower. I had been around these islands dozens of times aboard my dad's boat but had never found them quite as interesting as they were this morning.

I watched a lobster boat glide through the water and approach the cove from Isle Au Haut's main harbor. As the boat passed the spindle between our island and Kimball Island I could see the name *Danita* on the bow in large black letters. The *Danita* entered the cove and slowed to a drift. I watched as the captain reached over the side with a short gaff hook and pulled a yellow-and-red buoy from the water to the boat. Next he ran the line trailing from the buoy through a block that hung on the end of a short davit mounted on the outside bulkhead of his boat's small house. He drew the line from the block into the steel plates of his hydraulic pot hauler. Seconds later a wooden lobster trap broke the surface and came to rest against the hull of the *Danita*. The captain yanked the trap onto the gunwale of the boat and slid it aft a bit, where his helper opened it up.

The helper in the stern of the boat appeared to be a boy not much bigger than myself. The boy picked the lobsters from the trap, tossing the small ones back into the water and placing the larger ones on a table beside him. He then baited the trap with some type of dead fish, closed the top of the trap, and turned to the table where he had placed the big lobsters. While the boy measured the lobsters and stretched rubber bands around their claws, the captain shifted the boat's engine back into gear and pushed the trap over the side and into the water, allowing the line to pay out over the rail of the boat. The buoy splashed in behind the trap and line, and the boat turned and headed toward the lighthouse. The captain waved in my direction with a smile. I was thrilled and surprised with the wave, and waved back with enthusiasm that shook my chunky frame. Just then I was startled by a voice behind me. "Hi, Captain Jack!"

The familiar voice carried across the cove to the *Danita*. I turned and looked to see two small figures waving their arms at the boat. My younger brother and sister, five-year-old twins, sat perched on top of a ledge like a couple of seagulls. I climbed up the ledge and joined the twins, the three of us watching the *Danita* make her way to the next yellow-and-red buoy. "Do you know them?" I asked, my gaze fixed on the hauling of the next trap.

"Yup. They got three keepers out of that last trap. Only had two yesterday," answered my little sister, Bif. Bif, short for Elizabeth, was the talkative one of the twins and usually answered for both herself and our brother, Charlie. Charlie nodded his blond curly head as if confirming Bif's lobster tally, his bright blue eyes intensely watching the picking of the second trap. "Wow, looks like four good ones this time! Didn't they only get one there yesterday?" Bif asked of Charlie.

Still nodding and staring, Charlie answered in his usual one syllable. We watched as the trap was baited and pushed back into the water, disappearing in the wake behind the boat. The *Danita* turned and went around the point of land where Point Robinson Lighthouse stood, leaving behind a puff of white exhaust and a wake that quietly rolled its way to the shore at our feet.

With the boat now out of our view, Bif focused on me. "That was Jack MacDonald and his son Danny. You know, Danny from the softball games? Jack waves to us every day, and we count lobsters. He catches a lot more than the other lobstermen," she explained.

"A lot more," Charlie echoed as he made his way down the ledge and onto the beach, where he found a small tidal pool. Charlie crouched at the edge of the pool and stared into it as if he were seeing all the way to China. After thorough examination he looked up at Bif and me with a grin and reported, "Four crabs! Eleven periwinkles!" He stood now and peered down the beach, focusing on a much larger tidal pool. Hopping from rock to rock, Charlie made his way to the bigger pool and, wading in up to his knees, began his count again.

Below me on the beach, Bif was struggling with a bunch of mussels. She pulled the mussels away from the rocks where they had attached themselves. As she freed them from their tangled mess she laid them singly on a flat rock beside her. As the top of the rock filled with mussels I asked, "Does Mom know you two are down here alone?"

"We're not alone, we're with you. She said for you to keep an eye on us and don't let us get our sneakers wet again," Bif answered, pulling another dark blue shell from between two stones and laying it with the others.

I laughed, looking at Charlie, who was now up to his waist in the salt water. "I guess it's a little late for the sneakers."

Bif shifted her attention from the mussels to Charlie and shouted, "You better get out of that water. Mom's gonna be mad."

Charlie said "Yup" and climbed out of the giant puddle. He sloshed and dripped his way back up the rocky beach, joining Bif by the pile of mussels. Grabbing a stone about the size of a baseball, Charlie began smashing the blue shells Bif had so carefully laid out. Fully expecting Bif to scream or run home to tattle, I watched in amazement as she picked up one of the squashed mussels to feel the gooey yellow mush insides with the fingers of both hands.

"What are you doing?" I asked, surprised that my usually squeamish little sister would touch the guts of anything.

"Looking for pearls. We found two yesterday. Makes sixteen all together."

"Yup. Sixteen," echoed Charlie as he broke open the last of the shells.

While the twins busied themselves with their rituals and counting games, my attention returned to the water outside the cove. I looked as far to seaward as I could, beyond the islands, out into the middle of the bay. I was sure there was something out there for me; I could feel it. There were many things to see, but they were all just over the horizon, just beyond my sight. I squinted and strained to see farther, but it was no use. I knew instinctively that the ocean had stories to tell me, all I needed to do was listen. Intrigued, I searched the beach at my feet and found a shell that had been vacated by a hermit crab. Putting the shell to my ear, I listened to the empty, hollow, ringing sound. There was a pattern to the ringing that reminded me of the surf on the ledges when the wind blows. There was something else, though, something faint and far out to sea.

Clasping the shell to my ear and scanning the horizon across the bay, I found myself lost in a most vivid daydream. I imagined boats and fish and faraway islands. I harpooned whales, jigged for cod, and sailed clear across the Atlantic Ocean before my dream was interrupted by the tide coming in around me. The twins had already found some higher ground up the beach and were scratching their names into a small patch of wet sand with sticks. Unwilling to let my daydream evaporate, I asked, "Anyone want to go fishing?"

"I do," answered Charlie, dropping his driftwood pencil.

"Me, too! Aren't you going to play in the woods today?" asked Bif.

"No." I smiled. "Today I'm going to sea."

And go to sea I did, every chance I got for the next twenty years. Rarely did a day leave me ashore. I rowed until I inherited an antique outboard motor; I putted around the cove in the skiff until I had courage enough to "borrow" my Dad's 40-foot powerboat, at an age when most kids contemplate stealing the family car. I fished, mostly with hook and line, for mackerel and pollock, and experimented with nets and makeshift harpoons. Fishing my way through college, I made my first Grand Banks trip at the age of nineteen aboard the *Walter Leeman*. My primary job was cooking, and although I disliked the galley chores, I liked the money. It wasn't until a fellow crew member hit the bunk with a back injury that I was allowed to work the deck, work I enjoyed for years. While harpooning, I was spotting the majority of the fish before Alden or any of my shipmates, and because I was experienced at running my dad's boat, became the *Walter Leeman*'s helmsman.

By the time I graduated from college I had outlasted the original crew members I had started with, most of whom moved on to boats of their own, and became first mate by attrition. Promising my parents that I would postpone law school for just one year, I became a full-time fisherman. One year turned into sixteen. After I had been working as mate aboard the *Walter Leeman* for four years,

Alden bought a second boat, the *Gloria Dawn*, and gave me my first opportunity as captain. I learned the bulk of what I know about at-sea emergency repairs and catching swordfish in my three years at the wheel of the *Gloria Dawn*; it was an expensive education in many ways, and it nearly put Alden in the poorhouse. I have fished on a number of different boats involved in a number of different fisheries, learning something from each and every experience; I am still learning today.

Being a woman hasn't been a big deal. I never anticipated problems stemming from being female, and never encountered any. I have been surprised, even embarrassed, by the number of people who are genuinely amazed that a woman might be capable of running a fishing boat. Frankly, I'm amazed that they're amazed. People, women in particular, are generally disappointed when they learn that I have not suffered unduly from being the only woman in what they perceive to be a man's world. I might be thick-skinned—or just too damn busy working to worry about what others might think of me.

5

THE MEN

"Crew problems" is the phrase spoken in reference, aboard a fishing vessel, to anything from seasickness to homesickness, but is most often used to describe problems stemming from laziness and personality conflicts. If there is a crew of even one person, crew problems are assured. Some problems of the crew are easily solved, the captain nipping them in the bud, while others persist, compromising morale the duration of the trip. Thirty days is a long time to expect six individuals cohabiting a 100-foot space, working long hours, under less than fair conditions, deprived of sleep, to get along amicably, especially when the six are fishermen. I certainly did not expect it this trip, and would not be disappointed.

It was peaceful in the wheelhouse that first night as the *Hannah Boden* cut through the flat calm water on her easterly heading. The only indication of human life from the galley below drifted up to the bridge as invisible clouds of fresh cigarette smoke and onion. Ringo must be up and cooking dinner, I thought. The scents of tobacco and onion formed one single unique odor. Smoking was forbidden inside the fo'c'sle and was permitted only on deck. The crew, all smokers, ignored the rule, and I ignored the fact that they were breaking it. I asked only that they please refrain from using cigarettes in the wheelhouse and in their bunks, smoke being capable of damaging electronic equipment, and smoking in bed being one of the top causes of shipboard fires. Tolerating the smoking of cigarettes in the galley was something that I could concede to the crew.

The last daylight was long gone, and the screens of the electronics shone intensely in the blackness. I walked around and dimmed the screens to their lowest adjustments, stopping to look out the rear windows at the phosphorescence in our wake. The night was totally dark and moonless, and luminescence sparkled only where the surface had been agitated by the boat, a reaction of some sort, brief and bright flickers of light the color of the stars. I have never known the scientific explanation for this phenomenon, and was happy simply to observe it. When I'm staring into a fire, I don't need to understand the mathematical formulas and chemical reactions to appreciate the beauty; perhaps it is the *not* understanding that keeps me in awe.

My private light show was interrupted when Ringo entered the wheelhouse, minus cigarette.

"Hi, Ma! Are you hungry?" He cocked his blond-mop-covered head to one side. Ringo had referred to me as "Ma" on a previous trip as a joke. The name had stuck. Although I disliked it from the start, I had been called much worse, so being referred to as Ma was something I tolerated from those who dared.

"Hi. Yeah, I'm starving just about to death up here. I haven't eaten all day."

"I can see that." Ringo grabbed the nearly empty Lay's bag and gave it a shake.

"Well, except for some chips, and fish cakes, eggs, toast, and a few chocolate bars. Hey, something sure smells good. What's cooking?"

"Spaghetti, spaghetti with sausage and meatballs. I'm waiting for the water to boil for the pasta. Would you like your salad now?"

"Yes. I would, please."

"Italian?"

"Yes, please."

"You got it, Ma. Coming right up." He disappeared down the gangway.

Cooking aboard a boat is no easy task. But the better the food, the better the morale; and Ringo is the best cook I've ever had. The crew and I help ourselves to lunch and break-fast whenever time and weather conditions permit. Dinner, being the one formal meal of the day, is prepared by whoever is designated cook for the trip. The evening meal is some-thing we all look forward to, and with Ringo aboard, it is always a treat. He takes pride in his work; some of his specialties include prime rib, baked stuffed shrimp, and filet of sole with crabmeat stuffing. Along with quality, quantity is also never lacking. One time Ringo put together a lasagna with so much ground beef and sausage it weighed over 20 pounds. He was so proud of his monstrosity that he insisted I take a picture of him with it. He put on a clean shirt and posed on deck, down on one knee with the pan held out in front of him like a trophy fish. When there is this type of lighthearted play, it usually is a sign of a crew free of problems.

Through the years, I have experienced some of the worst cooking I could ever have imagined possible, and these times of bad food were also periods of serious crew problems, something I never considered coincidence. The most horrendous dish I can remember was a tuna casserole. When I questioned the cook about what the hell he had done to it to make it so gross, he replied that he didn't know and that actually the recipe was quite simple and his own invention. The entire casserole consisted of only two ingredients: canned tuna fish and Ruffles potato chips. After baking for three hours, it was so dry we couldn't begin to eat it, so we tossed it overboard. Poor fishing and low morale followed us for the next three days, and the casserole took the blame. This particular cook was a truck driver by trade, and he revealed to the rest of us, at about mid-trip, that he intended to fish only this one trip, the proceeds from which he would use to buy his own eighteen-wheeler. (Yes, he was clueless.) By the end of the trip I had convinced him that he should not have lied about his extensive fishing and cooking experience, because it had become painfully obvious to us all, once we left the dock, that he had never done either and that he would be lucky to receive enough compensation to purchase a skateboard. But he was right about one thing: That was his only trip.

I often worked as cook aboard the *Walter Leeman* when I first started fishing. I never enjoyed cooking in good weather, and thoroughly despised it in bad. My most vivid memories of cooking include numerous times when upon opening the refrigerator all of its contents cascaded onto the galley floor and rolled back and forth across the linoleum with the motion of the boat, sour cream lids opening, pickle jars shattering. Apples were always among the last to be recaptured, and were never quite the same after their brief moments of freedom. As captain, I always insist that the crew keep the galley floor swept clean, as most meals will have at least one ingredient hit the deck before being served.

Preparing meals for six people for thirty days can be quite a chore, and most cooks are expected to carry a full load of deck responsibilities as well. It is absolutely expected and acceptable to hear the cook screaming profanities while getting a meal together in rough seas. If there are no obscenities heard, there is probably no cooking going on, in which case all shipmates fend for themselves. Peanut butter sandwiches and Pop-Tarts are common heavy weather meals.

Ringo returned to the bridge with my tossed salad. As he handed it to me, he asked if I had made the night's watch bill.

"No, not yet. I'll start the watches at ten; everyone should be in pretty good shape by then."

"Yes. Everyone is fine. I'll take the first watch."

I had no trouble finishing the salad. As I ate the last bite of lettuce, the spaghetti appeared. The *Hannah Boden*'s dinner dishes are Pyrex pie plates, which are better suited for boat use than ordinary flat plates; the rim keeps the food from sliding onto the table or into laps in rough seas. Standard procedure aboard most boats is for the cook to relieve the captain of all wheelhouse duties during meals, allowing the captain to join the crew at the galley table. I usually prefer to take my meals in the wheelhouse. On the occasions when I do eat with the crew, I find myself inhaling my food, worried about what I might be missing by not paying attention to the radios on the bridge. At this time in the evening, the boats that are on the fishing grounds are busy setting out. Captains use this time to share information about numbers of fish caught that day, what their location is, what water temperature they found most productive, when they will be heading to the dock, weather conditions and forecasts, and other conversation that could answer questions that I might have and help me to form a strategy. Most captains participate in the exchange; all captains listen.

I took my dirty dishes down to the galley and laid them in the sink. Someone had scribbled a schedule for washing dishes on a paper plate and taped it to a cupboard door. Charlie would wash them tonight. The guys sat smoking and talking across the galley table, and a VCR movie played on the TV screen in the background. Glancing at the screen, I exclaimed, "*Lonesome Dove* again?" Every time I had entered the galley last trip, if anything was on the screen, it was *Lonesome Dove*. The crew knew the entire three tapes by heart and had acted out whole scenes on deck.

"We were just discussing something down here, Ma. Maybe you can clear it up for us," Ringo said, putting his cigarette out in a makeshift tinfoil ashtray.

"What might that be?"

"We heard a rumor that you don't like TV." It was obvious to me that they were all holding back laughter.

"Well, it's not that I don't like it," I said. "I don't get much opportunity to watch it."

"Actually, what we heard was that you don't like television sets."

Now I knew what Ringo was getting at. "Actually, what you heard was that I once threw a fire ax through a TV screen when I felt that I was not getting my crew's undivided attention."

"That's exactly what we heard. Is it true?"

"I guess if you pay attention, you'll never find out."

I left the galley to check the engine room. When I returned to the bridge I thought about the TV incident. I thought about how my first captain, Alden, pitted himself against the crew to keep them unified. Alden always figured that as long as the crew was mad at him, they would leave one another alone, lessening the chances of the usual crew problems. I grabbed my notebook and pen, and wrote out the watch bill for the night. My standard watch bill is a list of the names of the crew members who will stand a wheel watch for the night, with the times of each of their watches and a list of any special instructions that might be needed for any particular night. Basically, the watch stander is responsible for keeping the boat on course, checking the engine room, and avoiding collision with other vessels or landmasses.

Some captains leave it up to the crew to determine who will stand watch and when, the only instruction being "Don't wake me up." I have been told by crew members of mine who have experienced this type of loose and unstructured style that it often leads to someone's feeling cheated and eventually to arguments, or even fistfights, as the trip wears on and sleep is in short supply. A strict watch bill prepared by the captain is one less bone of contention among the crew.

WATCHES

Ringo	10:00–11:30
Charlie	11:30–1:00
Kenny	1:00–2:30
Carl	2:30–4:00
Peter	4:00–5:30

PLEASE CHECK THE ENGINE ROOM EVERY 30 MINUTES.

KEEP THE BOAT ON COURSE WITH PLOTTER.

WAKE ME IF ANYTHING COMES WITHIN TWO MILES ON RADAR, OR IF YOU HAVE ANY QUESTIONS OR PROBLEMS.

THANKS. GOOD NIGHT.

I rotate the watch positions every night so that the last man on the list takes the first watch the following night. First and last watches are most desirable because whatever sleep you do get is not interrupted in the middle. Ringo relieved me at ten o'clock sharp, and I turned on the weather fax (the machine that prints out weather maps) before crawling into my bunk. It seemed I had just closed my eyes when I heard a voice.

"Good morning, Linda." Peter poked his head through my stateroom's doorway, waking me to our second day of steaming. "Five-thirty, time to get up."

I stood and looked out of my porthole, a round window about 12 inches in diameter. It wasn't quite daylight yet. The boat snapped quickly to port, and I lurched forward, catching myself before hitting the bulkhead. The wind had picked up from the south. It wasn't bad, maybe 20 or 25 knots, but enough to liven the motion of the boat to the point of needing the stabilizing birds lowered into the water. "Hey Peter, wake up the other guys and ask Kenny to put the birds in, please," I said, and stepped into my head to brush my teeth. I enjoyed having my own head, or bathroom, adjoining my stateroom. It is one of the fringe benefits of being captain, and insured me the privacy I needed as the only female on the boat. The *Hannah Boden*'s captain's head is comprised of a white porcelain toilet bowl with saltwater flush, a small sink, a mirror, and a shower stall. Both the sink and shower are plumbed with hot and cold running fresh water, all the comforts of home. The crew's head is down below, opposite the galley, and has two sinks, a shower, a toilet, and a clothes washer and dryer. Although we were equipped with a desalinator, a machine that makes fresh water from salt water, we had to be careful about using the washing machine, as it used 50 gallons for each load, and "water makers" are known to be temperamental. The *Hannah Boden* carries over 10,000 gallons of fresh water, which is enough for a trip as long as everyone uses it economically.

I stepped out into the wheelhouse and immediately looked into the radar. A clear screen showed no company for a radius of 12 miles. The plotter showed the boat slightly north of our desired course line, and all engine instruments indicated that everything was normal. When I heard the *click* of the electric hydraulic pump and the loud humming of the oil being forced through the hydraulic system, I slowed the boat to an idle as Kenny maneuvered the valves behind the wheelhouse, lowering the birds from the ends of the outriggers to where they swam 20 feet below the surface. With the birds in position, I returned the throttle to 1,600 RPMs and turned to the chart table to check our present position. With the birds in, the *Hannah Boden* was as steady as she is in flat calm.

The GPS indicated 43 degrees 03 minutes north and 66 degrees 17 minutes west. The lines of latitude run horizontally across the chart, measuring distance north and south of the equator, and longitude lines, which measure distance east and west of the prime meridian, running through Greenwich, England, run vertically. These two sets of lines intersect each other at angles close to 90 degrees, forming a grid on the chart. I found the point at which 43° 03' N and 66° 17' W intersected on the chart, marked it with a pencil dot as our present position, and labeled it with the date and time. This new dot was about an inch southwest of the southwestern tip of Nova Scotia, 1 inch being equal to around 36 nautical miles on this particular chart. (Measuring daily progress in inches takes some getting used to.)

I searched for the parallel rulers in the drawer below the chart table. Pulling the clear plastic rulers from the drawer, I laid them on the chart, sliding them so that the edge of one ruler connected our present position to another pencil dot to the east, south of Sable Island, that would act as my next waypoint. "Walking" the hinged rulers across the chart so as not to change the angle of the straightedge, I moved them to the nearest compass rose and read our desired course from the numbers of calibration around the rose, which is a circular printing of the points of a true compass, north being straight up. I positioned one edge of the rulers so that it lay across the center of the bagel-sized rose, and read the number at the outside edge of the rose where the same ruler edge intersected it, finding my desired true course to be 82. The chart indicated 18 degrees of westerly magnetic variation for this area, so I added 18 to the 82, for a magnetic course of 100 degrees. The deviation of the *Hannah Boden*'s compass for 100 is 3 east, so I subtracted the 3 to give me a desired compass course of 97. To achieve my desired true course of 82, I must steer a compass course of 97.

Returning to the front of the bridge, I watched the compass that was mounted on the console in front of the large stainless steel steering wheel, or helm. The compass is about the size and shape of a basketball cut in half, the flat surface against the console. I peered through the glass dome at the black disk with its white numbers of calibration floating in the clear liquid as the lubber (fixed) line wiggled slowly back and forth around 92. I turned the knob on the autopilot clockwise a bit, to add 5 degrees to our heading. I returned to the chart table and, with my dividers, measured the distance on the chart between our present position and the next waypoint, below Sable Island.

Spanning the legs of the dividers from point to point and holding them against the latitude scale on the horizontal border of the chart gave me the distance in nautical miles. One minute of latitude is equal to 1 nautical mile, and 1 degree of latitude is 60 minutes, or 60 miles. We had approximately 290 miles to go to reach the pencil mark south of Sable Island, a little less than a day and a half at our present speed. Keying the appropriate numbers into the GPS, I let it calculate electronically what I had just done the old-fashioned way. It took two seconds to check my navigation, and I found the numbers very close.

I relaxed in my chair and examined the weather maps that had been printed through the night. The surface analysis showed a weak low off Cape Cod approaching at 15 knots. A 20-knot wind flag from the south confirmed the breeze we had this morning, and it looked like we might get some heavy rain as the low passed by during the day. Isobars forming the back side of the low were closer together than those forming the leading edge, indicating an increase in wind, but not enough to bother the 100-foot *Hannah Boden*.

The smell of fresh coffee ascended from the galley, and my stomach growled as I checked out the sea surface temperature chart. This map gave me a rough idea of temperature breaks on the fishing grounds; I could judge from it where the bulk of the fleet would be found. Where the edges of separate pieces of hot and cold water lay adjacent to one another, large temperature gradients called "breaks" are found. The most desirable pieces of water, "berths" or "sets," would be where the hottest water pushed farthest to the north and formed the tightest breaks. Personally, I like corners. Where the main temperature break makes large and definite direction changes, the edge forms a corner, and that is where I like to be. In recent trips I had fished a corner that forms in the vicinity of 45 degrees north and 45 degrees west. Below this corner, the edge and current run to the northeast, and beyond it both run due east. My favorite berth starts below the corner and runs away from it to the southwest. The nearly 3 knots of tide takes my 40 miles of gear into and around the corner where the east end straightens out east and west. I had had such good fishing in this area that I was certain it would not be available for me this trip.

Someone else would have staked his claim on my favorite spot.

Both setting and hauling are done against the tide, in order to hold the berth for the next set, not losing too much ground to the east at the hands of the swift current. Jockeying for position and aggressively holding a 40-mile-long piece of the break is imperative if you want to have any degree of success. Everyone tries to be where the biggest and most fish are being caught; usurping a few miles from either end of a good berth is done when allowed. A captain must have an understanding of the shape and movement of the various ocean features, such as eddies and the Gulf Stream, and be forceful to hold a lucrative berth. It is generally understood that if given an inch, anyone will take a mile. I know that I must sound like a bitch on the radio to the other captains when fighting to retain my 40-mile slot, but I learned the hard way not to budge for anyone. The meek may inherit the Earth, but they'll never get my piece of the ocean. In four days the game would begin, and we would be racing the clock, the tide, the moon, and the rest of the fleet. He who catches the most the fastest wins.

It was now daylight, but so overcast that I hadn't had the pleasure of watching the sun rise. The sky was dull gray, the ocean flat black with flashes of stark white as the tops of the low choppy seas broke into short tumbling curls and then fell to black again. People unfamiliar with the ocean imagine it as always blue, but depending on the weather conditions, it can appear to be many colors. Steady rain fell, the drops leaving ripples in the smooth black patches between the whitecaps. I folded the fax paper accordion style and tossed it onto the console in front of the chair.

I grabbed a paperback book and opened it to where I had stopped reading a few days before. An observer might think that I was enjoying the book, but I was actually just going through the motions of reading it. My eyes went back and forth from line to line, and I knew when to turn the page, but my mind was not on the writing and the story couldn't hold my interest. I wondered how many fish we would catch this trip, and worried about what weather we would have to endure, what the price of swordfish would be when we returned to Gloucester at the end of September, and what form the inevitable crew problems would take.

"Good morning, Ma!" Kenny stepped from behind my chair to the front of the wheelhouse, where he stood beside me and held out a steaming cup of coffee. A native Newfoundlander, Kenny spoke with an Irish brogue and often used expressions that were unfamiliar to the rest of us. It was fun to listen to him talk. His bright hair fell over his forehead and hid the lumps that I had noticed yesterday. It is a well-known fact that all fishermen are liars, and at the age of twenty-two, Kenny was already the king. The rest of us had decided that Kenny must have started fishing while still in the womb to have done half of what he claims to have done. He had been on the *Hannah Boden* since the age of seventeen. Prior to that age he had allegedly fished on another U.S. swordboat, a Japanese long-liner, a bluefin tuna boat, a couple of scallopers, every gillnetter in Newfoundland, a few drag-gers, and had gone seal hunting aboard a boat his grandfather ran, probably clubbing baby seals while still in his diapers. The only thing that topped Kenny's sea stories were his tales of hunting. He was absolutely sober and straightfaced when he spun a yarn about shooting 500 ducks in one day. I am not a duck hunter, but I was certainly impressed. Sto-rytelling is a valuable skill for a crew member to possess when spending thirty days at sea, and Kenny was a master.

"Carl is shoveling ice," Kenny told me, "and we'll start on the gear work as soon as we've eaten. I'll wait until this afternoon to switch generators, okay?"

"Okay, take the ammeter down with you. Check the batteries when you put the beepers together. We should have four spares up in the forepeak."

Kenny opened the top of the bench seat at the back of the wheelhouse where I stored odds and ends such as electrical tape, duct tape, flash-light batteries, and rolls of fax paper. He pulled out the ammeter and went back below. Kenny had made every Grand Banks trip with me since I had started on the *Hannah Boden*, and I depended on him heavily. He had taken over the engineer duties for me, doing the maintenance in the engine room while we were at sea. The switching of generators was done once a day. We had two generators, each of which was run every other day, alternating days so that one engine ran at all times. Before Kenny took over for me, I tried to do everything myself, and often hurried through my engine room chores. Bob Brown had warned me more than once that being in a hurry and taking shortcuts would eventually, in his words, "bite me in the ass."

I didn't like the heat and noise of the engine room, and once made a terrible mistake by being careless. While changing the oil in one of the generators, I accidentally pumped the oil from the other generator while it was running at full RPMs by forgetting to close a valve. I had also apparently neglected to turn on the alarms that automatically shut the engine down when the oil pressure is too low or the temperature is too high. The generator ran itself to death with no oil, blowing a hole in the block the size of a grapefruit and catching on fire. The engine was rebuilt to the tune of $25,000, a truly expensive bite on the ass; after that I relinquished all at-sea maintenance to Kenny, who seemed far more conscientious than I.

I also relied on Kenny to take care of the fish hold. As "hold man" Kenny was responsible for packing the fish in the saltwater ice. The fish are first chilled in one section of the hold, their body cavities stuffed with ice to bring their temperature down. Then, in the evening, while setting out, Kenny would pack the already chilled fish into pens, also called "bins," which are small areas of the hold sectioned off with penboards (two-by-sixes painted white). The fish are laid horizontally and stacked vertically, with the largest ones on the bottom, and each individual fish is totally surrounded by and buried in ice. Once fish are packed, they don't see the light of day again until unloaded at the dock. Kenny took excellent care of the fish, and we have received many compliments on quality from wholesalers.

Shortly after Kenny left the wheelhouse, Ringo appeared with two sandwiches wrapped in paper towels. I thanked him and placed the sandwiches in my lap. Ringo scanned the horizon through the front windows. "The weather's a little snotty this morning. What's the forecast?"

I took a big bite of the first sandwich and spoke with my mouth full, proving that I had finally managed to forget every single table manner that my mother had ever taught me. "The map is right there," I said, pointing to the folded fax paper with my sandwich. "It should be about like this, maybe a little more wind before it drops out late this afternoon. It's moving pretty fast. We may get a look at the sun before it sets tonight."

Ringo reached for the paper, and as he examined the surface analysis, resumed the conversation in what seemed to be a more serious tone than is usual for him. "I hate to be a rat, but Carl and Peter are about to come to blows."

"I noticed a personality conflict last trip, but thought they were over it by now. As long as they both do their jobs, it doesn't affect the rest of us, right?"

"You don't have to listen to it. You're up here," Ringo said, still looking at the weather map.

"Well, I can't make them like each other." I thought I sounded a bit defensive.

Ringo tossed the map back onto the console and looked me in the eye. "Among other endearments, Carl has been calling Peter 'filthy nigger.' I don't know if that has any effect on you, but it sure does me."

"Jesus." I put the uneaten sandwich on the console. The thought of Carl's directing the word *nigger* at his shipmate and my crewman gave me a sick feeling in the pit of my stomach. "I guess I am insulated from you guys up here. I had no idea it was this far out of hand. Well, thanks for bringing it to my attention. I'll put an end to it."

"I know you will. Peter must be getting tired of turning the other cheek. He's going to explode, and when he does, Carl may get hurt."

"Crew problems. I hate this shit. I hate it more than hurricanes and slow fishing. I've never had to deal with a racial problem before, but I guess I'm about to learn how. This sucks."

"That's why you get the big money, Ma."

"That's why I'm on the pointy end," I said, referring to the bow, as opposed to the square

85

stern end, where the crew spends a great deal of their time. It was a familiar exchange between Ringo and me, but didn't do much to lighten the atmosphere. Ringo left, saying that he would help Kenny with the beepers, and I sat staring out the window and wondering how this situation would best be handled.

I had witnessed fistfights before, but that was different. One could understand how six exhausted people stuck in each other's faces for thirty days might exhibit an occasional flaring of tempers and a quick flurry of punches. It happens, and I've never seen it amount to anything more than a bloody nose. I'm not a masochist, and have never considered stepping between two men who are throwing ham-sized fists at each other. There is never much warning for these physical outbursts, so I have always had to deal with the participants after the fact, after the frustration and anger has dissipated. I have learned that the best deterrent to a repeat performance is to threaten the men with, as Alden would say, "a hit where it hurts...right in the pocketbook." Just the threat of levying fines that can be deducted from paychecks has always been enough to keep everyone in line. Forewarned is forearmed. Ringo had warned me, and it was now my responsibility to defuse the situation before it got any hotter. The only question was, how? Would the threat of financial sanctions be enough? I hoped so.

I couldn't help but think about what an odd group we all comprised, the crew and I.

Except that we all made our livings at sea, we didn't have much else in common with one another. As a group, the six of us spanned generations, gender, race, religion, and three nationalities. We ranged in age from nineteen to forty, Carl being the youngest and Charlie the oldest. Our roots stretched north and south, Kenny's being planted in Newfoundland, and Peter's in Grenada. Ringo and Charlie are both natives of Massachusetts, and Carl and I call Maine home. This crew and captain of the *Hannah Boden* were the epitome of stereotypical fishermen, the stereotype being that there is none. Fully aware of the diversity of fishermen, even I have been surprised at times.

While spending some time in the small town of Lincoln, Delaware, one winter, I met two of the most unlikely fishermen I had ever imagined possible. Pedaling a bicycle south on Route 113, I came to a tiny piece of water, not much bigger than a puddle, called Hudson Pond. On the embankment sat two elderly women, one black and one white, staring at the red-and-white "bobbers" that lay in the muddy-looking water midway down the fishing lines that dangled from the ends of their Zebco poles. Both women wore dresses, which I found odd. Something about the combination of dresses and fishing poles intrigued me, and I stopped pedaling. I watched as the white woman reeled in her line and cast again, and reeled and cast, repeatedly, until the black woman spoke sharply to her in a strong Southern accent. "Now, Hazel, you're not gonna catch anything if you don't leave it still for a minute. No fish are going to be fast enough to catch your worm." Hazel ignored her friend and continued reeling and casting.

I left my bicycle by the side of the road and joined the women in the grass. Hazel was quite friendly and struck up a conversation immediately upon seeing me. Unfortunately, I couldn't understand a word she said, but her friend was kind enough to translate for me. It became obvious to me that Hazel was mentally retarded and the other woman was her friend and caretaker. Between them on the grassy embankment they had a white plastic bucket that held half a dozen of the smallest yellow fish I had ever seen, "sunnies" they called them, and a coffee can full of dirt and earthworms that they used for bait. Hazel sputtered something unintelligible and held her fishing pole out to me, which the other woman translated. "She wants you to try. You ever caught a fish before?"

"No," I lied. I didn't think they would believe me if I told them that I was captain of a 100-foot swordfishing vessel and caught fish for a living; in fact, Hazel's friend might think she had found herself a second charge to take care of. "I would like to, though. Can you teach me?"

"Yes, child." The woman patiently and expertly taught me to bait the hook and cast out to the middle of the small pond. "Now we wait. Just watch that bobber. When it goes under, you got yourself a fish." The three of us sat in comfortable silence and watched the red-and-white floats in the brown water. My bobber bounced up and down a couple of times and then was jerked out of sight. Hazel clapped her hands and laughed wildly with excitement. "Reel it in, girl. Reel it right in. Easy now, that's it." The black woman coached me until the fish joined us in the grass, where it flipped around like all fish do when out of the water. "I'll take it off the hook for you. You can take it home for supper."

"Oh, no, thank you. I'm sure my boyfriend has supper planned," I said.

Hazel again spoke, and I wanted desperately to understand her. Her face was so kind, and her tone of voice so full of expression, but her syllables were badly jumbled. "She says you gotta take home your first fish." I wondered if she really understood Hazel or if her filling in the blanks was just a part of their friendship.

"Well, all right, Hazel. Thank you. It was nice meeting you both. Thanks for teaching me to fish." I took the fish in one hand and climbed onto my bicycle. Hazel hugged me and then waved as I pedaled off up the road. When I turned and looked back, Hazel was still waving, and I waved back with fish in hand. Hazel continued to wave until she faded out of sight in the distance behind me.

As my memory of the two women dimmed, my thoughts were interrupted by Bob Brown's voice on the SSB radio. "WQX six four seven to the *Hannah Boden*. Are you on here, Linda?"

I left the chair and grabbed the microphone, which hung from the overhead in the after part of the wheelhouse. I stood on a small carpeted platform that Bob had had built for me so that I could reach the radios and searchlight controls, which also hung from the overhead. "Whiskey Romeo Charlie five two four five. Good morning, Bob. Over."

"Hello, Linda. I'll bet you have rain there. Over."

"Roger. A little draft from the south and plenty of rain. Over."

"How is everything running, and what's your position? Over."

"Everything is fine. Forty-three oh five north and sixty-five fifty west. We've averaged ten knots so far. We didn't have to put the birds in until this morning. Over."

"Good enough. I'm going away for a couple of days and will call you on this frequency when I get home. Over."

"Okay, Bob. Talk to you then. Thanks for the check. Whiskey Romeo Charlie five two four five. 'Bye."

"See ya. WQX six four seven, clear with the *Hannah Boden*."

I placed the mike back in its bracket and

watched out the back windows as Kenny and Ringo worked in the rain on the beeper buoys. The beepers were set in a rack made from stainless steel pipe. Pieces of pipe were welded to form square openings just big enough to hold one buoy each. Each buoy had its own slot in the rack, similar to an egg in a carton. The rack was mounted on the deck just ahead of the three-sided steel structure called the "cart house." The cart house was open to the stern and acted as a weather break for the men and gear. Leaders were made and stored in plastic boxes the size of four-man Jacuzzis in the shelter of the cart house, the roof of which was greatly appreciated on a rainy day.

Beeper buoys are a critical part of longline gear. The buoy itself, which is painted red, stands about 3 feet high; the base of the buoy is a watertight steel canister and holds an electronic bundle that transmits radio signals that are received by the radio direction finder (RDF) in the wheelhouse of the boat. Each buoy has its own frequency, different from the others on the boat. The beeper buoys are attached to the fishing line as it is set out over the stern at intervals of about 3 1/2 miles. The piece of gear between two beepers is called a "section." A typical set for me would be ten to twelve sections, or 35 to 40 miles. A bright yellow flotation ring, or collar, fits around the top of the steel canister, placed in a way to keep the buoy upright and its 10-foot-long antenna in the air. Ringo and Kenny were busy screwing the antennas onto the buoys and connecting the wires from the antennas to the transmitting canisters. The buoys are kept turned off until just prior to going overboard to save the batteries, which are also in the canisters. I keep a list of the beepers' frequencies in the order that they are set, so if the line is parted-off mid-string, I can simply tune in the next beeper on the RDF and it will indicate the direction in which the remaining gear lies from the boat. Part-offs, or breaks in the mainline, are common, and are most often caused by tide, deep-draft ships, or large sharks. I slid open one of the back windows and called down to Kenny, "Let me know when you're ready to test them." Kenny nodded, waved, and went back to work.

Closing the window, I turned toward the front of the wheelhouse to find that Peter had entered without a sound. This tall and muscular man was quite an imposing figure as he stood ramrod stiff, his back to the console, his large arms folded across his chest. Peter was soft-spoken, with a rich West Indian accent. "There is something I would like to discuss with you," he said.

"I know about your problems with Carl, and I'm sorry. I intend to put an end to the name-calling."

"I am tempted to put my hands around his neck and squeeze. But he's just a boy, no match for me." Peter uncrossed his arms, holding up his hands as if for inspection. They looked like baseball gloves.

"He is young, and ignorant in a lot of ways. He quit school in the fourth grade and went to work digging clams. I'm sure he didn't meet many black people on the clam flats in Maine. I don't think he reads well. Can you imagine being illiterate? But, still...no excuse to be calling you 'nigger.'"

"'Nigger' doesn't bother me half as much as 'yard ape' and 'porch monkey.' Hey, I just wanted to make you aware of the situation so if something happens between Carl and me, you'll know why."

"No, Peter. That's not going to work. If you think that warning me that something may happen makes it okay, you are wrong."

"If he opens his mouth one more time, I'll—"

I interrupted before Peter had the chance to spell out for me what he had in mind for Carl. "I forbid you to lay one finger on that boy. And if you do, it will cost you a lot of money."

"You sound like an overprotective mother."

"I don't care what I sound like. I have a job to do. Filling this boat with fish and getting it back to Gloucester in one piece is my only priority. Unfortunately, I can't do it alone. I need for you guys to work together. I don't need crew problems. I will talk to Carl and hope that we can all focus on why we're here. You'll have the first leader box full by dinner, won't you?"

"Yes, I will. I have one question for you before I get to work. May I call you 'Ma'?"

"Shit, no one else has bothered to ask permission. Sure, you can call me anything you like. Ma is fine."

"Okay, thanks, Ma." Peter left an air of sadness behind as he descended the gangway and disappeared below. I didn't feel I had handled the problem very well, and realized I should have been more sympathetic. I wondered how to approach Carl, who had a chip on his shoulder and was stubborn beyond his years. Peter would listen to reason. I wasn't so sure about Carl. Just last trip I had boasted about my crew on the radio. I'd called them the best crew I had ever had, and said that they made my job easy and the trip enjoyable. Now, I thought, some of the same group were going to make my trip miserable. I remembered seven months back, to a time when I had the worst crew experience of all my years fishing; it made this trip's problem seem more easily surmountable.

Seven months before, in February, I'd had the *Hannah Boden* swordfishing the Caribbean for the winter. We unloaded our trips in San Juan, Puerto Rico, and it was while tied to the dock in San Juan that I got a hint of the horror show that was to soon follow. Tied up beside us was the *Stephanie Vaughn*, another U.S. swordboat enjoying the blazing sun and blue water for the winter season. My friend Jerry, who ran the *Stephanie Vaughn* at the time, stood with me on the deck of the *Hannah Boden*, and we made small talk while he waited for his crew to show up with the groceries for their next trip. "Do you have any diabetics on the boat?" Jerry asked.

I thought this a strange question, but answered honestly. "No, not that I know of. Why?" Jerry took me by the arm and led me over to the port rail, where he pointed down and between the boats. A used syringe floated in the water. "Jesus. I don't think that belongs to any of my guys. Probably someone off one of the boats ahead of us." I didn't like looking at the syringe, and returned to the center of the deck.

"Well, I just thought I'd ask," Jerry said, and shrugged his shoulders.

About one week into the next trip it became clear that Jerry might have known more than he had let on and that I certainly should have taken the syringe as a warning. It was a bright and beautiful Caribbean day, and we worked in shorts, T-shirts, and flip-flops as we pulled the gear from the water. We hauled aboard a magnificent double marker. Still alive, the 200-pound swordfish shimmered in purple, blue, and silver as it laid on the deck waiting to be dressed (cleaned). Fish must be cleaned immediately and not left in the sun, especially down in the Caribbean, where we even painted the asbestos deck tiles white to keep them from absorbing heat and melting the tar that is used to adhere them to the steel deck beneath.

As I drove the boat down the string of gear, continuing to bring it aboard, I became annoyed with the fact that nobody had started cleaning the fish. "Where's Chad?" I asked James, the man who worked beside me at the starboard rail.

"I don't know," he answered.

"Well, please go find him. We need to get that fish off the deck and into the ice." Chad was the "butcher," the crew member whose responsibility it was to clean all fish as they came aboard. It was unusual that all crew members were not on deck while hauling back, but I thought maybe Chad had gone in to use the head. James returned and said that Chad was not in the galley, the head, or his stateroom. I pulled the boat out of gear and walked back to the cart house, where the two other men were winding 30-fathom leaders onto hydraulic-powered spools called "leader carts."

"Do you guys know where Chad is?" No one knew. "Well, he has to be here somewhere. He didn't dive overboard. Come on, let's search the boat. Check all the bunks, the head, the engine room, the wheelhouse, the forepeak, everywhere." We all went in different directions in search of Chad, and all met back on deck a few minutes later. I was approaching panic. We had covered the entire boat. I thought he must have fallen overboard when no one was looking, and yelled to James to bring me a beeper buoy from the rack to mark this end of the gear. I would have to steam back in the direction from which we had come and hope to find Chad still alive and treading water.

Just as I was about to cut the mainline, one of the guys yelled, "Here he is!" Curled up in a tiny crawl space, and hidden by bundles of orange floats, lay Chad, who appeared to be fast asleep. I thought, What a strange time and place to take a nap.

"Hey, Chad," I screamed. "Get out here and clean this fish. What the hell are you doing in there anyway?" He stirred, and managed to crawl out onto the deck on all fours. I was horrified as I watched him try to stand up. James grabbed him and sat him down on the fish hold hatch cover, where he appeared to fall back to sleep, cradling his own arms and rocking back and forth slightly. I looked at the fish in the sun. The purple and blue had totally disappeared with the last ounce of life; even the huge eye was starting to dry out. Now I was mad. "Are you going to take care of this fish, or shall we eat it for lunch?" I shouted. Chad opened his eyes but seemed unable to focus on anything. He stumbled from the hatch cover and picked up the meat saw he would normally use to sever the fins and head from the fish. "It's about time," I said, and returned to the starboard rail and the controls for the boat and longline spool.

I put the boat back into gear and continued hauling the line onto the giant spool. The other men took their cues and returned to their various jobs. I hadn't hauled 50 fathoms when James asked, "Would you like me to clean that fish?" I knocked the boat out of gear and stopped the spool from spinning once again. I sat on the rail and watched Chad, who was still struggling with the first pectoral fin. He stood teetering on the deck, his head bobbing and wagging all over the place. He leaned down toward the fish, nearly fell over, and caught himself with one hand. It was like watching a reeling drunk in slow motion. He remained in a three-point stance as if gathering his concentration and strength for another stab with the saw. The sea was like a millpond, but Chad's actions indicated a full gale. The man could literally not stand up. James helped Chad to the hatch again, where he sat, a bit less wobbly than before. James started on the fish.

"What is wrong with you?" I asked Chad.

His voice was as distorted as his movements, but I understood him to say "I guess I don't have my sealegs yet."

"Bullshit! We've been out here for over a week, and it's flat-assed calm. Are you on drugs?" I was not surprised when Chad mumbled a denial. As James finished with the fish, I looked from Chad to the other two guys, neither of whom would look me in the eye; in fact, all three seemed quite interested in their own feet. With the exception of James, who had been working with me for years, Chad and the other two men had been strangers to me until just recently. "Jesus. I've got three druggies aboard here, don't I?" The men offered denials and continued to avoid eye contact with me. I thought if I had been wrongly accused of drug abuse, my response would have been adamant;

I would have been deeply insulted. I certainly would not have been hanging my head in shame and inspecting my toenails.

"Okay, I'm going to get the rest of this gear aboard and head for San Juan. Those of you who will not pass a drug test when we get there may as well pack your bags." We were less than forty-eight hours from the dock, and I knew that I could not continue working with this crew. After we arrived in San Juan, the three men shuffled up the dock with their seabags. They never looked back as I wished them good riddance.

My present crew might terrorize Gloucester when we're ashore, but they had always behaved as gentlemen in my presence. I liked these men and had come to think of them as friends. I put a tape in the stereo and listened to Bonnie Raitt's "Storm Warning" as I watched a massive low black cloud approach from the west. The storm cloud gained on us so quickly, I felt like I was watching time-lapse photography. As it neared I could see the sharp white peaks of steep waves under the cloud's leading edge. The wind increased in an instant as the darkness and driving rain overtook us, reducing the visibility to almost zero. I watched the strong southerly wind blow the beeper antennas from straight up to 45-degree angles.

A flash of lightning lit up the blackness for a fraction of a second and was followed by a clap of thunder so loud I felt it in my bones. I watched the five men turn the corner of the cart house one at a time and sprint up the deck for the fo'c'sle door. I heard the door open and slam shut and looked down the stairway to see the five men dripping in the companionway. Ringo shouted up, "We thought we would come in for lunch and work on lightsticks until the rain lets up."

"Are you afraid you might melt?" I teased.

"Easy question for you to ask. Up there, nice and dry, music blasting..."

"That's why I'm on the pointy end."

"That's why you get the big money, Ma."

Within the next thirty minutes the wind managed to increase to an intensity that made me realize that the weather map I had was worthless. The breeze that had whistled in the rigging that morning was now producing a loud hum as the stay-wires vibrated like giant guitar strings. The seas were mounting, and the height and weight of the waves caused me concern as they curled in over the starboard rail, filling the deck with water. The *Hannah Boden* rolled starboard to port, starboard to port, a little deeper each time. When she rolled far enough to dip the end of the port out-rigger, I declared it time to abandon our course and "round the boat up into it," or steer directly into the wind and sea, rather than running "side to it" any longer. I turned the autopilot 90 degrees to starboard, putting the bow into the waves, which were now being driven by 50 to 60 knots of screeching wind.

I slowed the engine to 1,000 RPMs to lessen the impact of the waves as they pounded the bow.

At one P.M., I marked our position on the chart, 43° 10' N and 64° 45' W. We had made almost 70 miles since five-thirty A.M., but were now only holding our position, as if jogging in place. There was no sense being in a hurry now. We were doing what was necessary to stay safe. Many boats that have gotten into serious trouble during storms have done so because of their refusal to abandon their course. The intense desire to go home keeps many men of the sea from ever getting there, when a homeward course takes their boats along a beam to the wind, a dangerous path.

The *Hannah Boden*'s bow lurched into the seas and sent heavy spray that hit the wheelhouse windows with a *whomp*. The wind was now blowing the tops off the waves before they could crest, leaving white streaks of foam on the surface. Given time, this wind would build a treacherous sea, and I prayed that the low would move beyond us before nightfall. Everything seems more dramatic in the dark, when you can't see the next nasty wave and brace yourself before it smashes onto the bow. In the dark you can hear and feel the reality, but the visual horror is left to the imagination.

By five P.M. the conditions had neither improved nor worsened, and I was weary from bracing myself, holding on, and trying to stay in the saddle for the duration of this wild ride. I thanked God when the barometer finally started its slow climb, indicating an increase of pressure, a sure sign that relief was in the near future. By six P.M. the wind had switched to northwest and quickly diminished to a light breeze. Soon the sea had mellowed to a long and low swell that delivered an occasional halfhearted slap to the side of the steel hull, which was once again heading to the fishing grounds. The northwest breeze, or "clearing wind," had managed to live up to its name. Every pelting drop of rain and every black cloud had been blown to the east, where they were no doubt tormenting some other fishermen.

Carl skipped up the stairs and stood beside me looking out the back windows at the blue sky just before sunset. I had completely forgotten about my crew problem and was waiting to watch the sun disappear when Carl's presence jogged my memory. Not much of a conversationalist, Carl often entered and exited the wheelhouse without so much as a peep. He looked at the GPS and then at the chart, finding our position with the tip of an index finger. I had taught Carl the basics of navigation and was amazed at how much he'd absorbed in a short time. I never had to tell Carl anything more than once. Thin and wiry, resembling a young Richard Gere, with an attitude to match, he had mastered all deck skills and moved with a youthful quickness, yet worked with a mature accuracy.

I knew that Carl would never initiate a conversation with me and that I would have to do most of the talking, but I wasn't sure where to begin. Carl grabbed the sharpening stone that I kept on the chart table, sat on the top step of the gangway, and began sharpening the knife that he kept in the sheath on his hip at all times. I watched as he pushed the blade slowly the length of the gray surface, and thought how I loved the sound of the steel against stone. When done properly, as Carl did, the rhythm of the repeated strokes created a cadence so clean and crisp that the sound alone was sharp enough to cut. "I understand that you and Peter have a problem," I said.

"I fuckin' hate him." Carl's eyes, the color of melted chocolate, never left the stone.

"Why?"

"He stinks."

"You dislike him because he stinks?"

"And he's lazy." Carl felt the edge of the knife with his thumb.

"Carl, we're all lazy compared to you."

"He doesn't do his share." He looked up at me for the first time since he'd entered the wheelhouse.

"Well, I think that's for me to determine, not you." I got no response, so I continued. "I am happy with the job Peter does. No one else wants to spend twenty hours a day back there in the cart house, repairing and coiling leaders." Still no response. "I have warned Peter that if you provoke him into a fight, he stands to lose his paycheck."

103

"I ain't afraid of him."

"Are you afraid of losing your paycheck?"

"Nope. Money don't mean much to me; it's only paper. You told me when I first came aboard if I wanted to go fishing just for the money that I should stay ashore. I like fishing, and that's why I'm here."

"Well, great. You're not afraid of getting the shit beaten out of you, and you don't care about your paycheck. I'm fresh out of threats. What the hell can I say to you to get you to keep your mouth shut and stop with the nasty names?"

"You could just ask me to stop. I've never ignored anything you've told me in the past, have I?"

What a relief. I couldn't believe I had fretted about this all day. "Gee, why didn't I think of that? Carl, I think I owe you an apology. I assumed I would have to coerce you into behaving like a human being. Shit, I'll even ask you nicely. Please stop calling Peter names. It's not nice and it makes me sick."

"Okay." Carl stood and put the sharpening stone back on the chart table and his knife back into the sheath. As he went down the stairs he yelled back over his shoulder, "Ringo says dinner will be ready in about an hour. Pork chops."

If Carl lived up to his word, and I believed that he would, the crew problems hadn't amounted to much.

6

MUG-UP

When I first started fishing, some of the
crustiest of the old-timers had me convinced
that they could predict the weather without
the use of electronics. Aches and pains were
often the forerunners of an approaching low-
pressure system. If arthritis flared up in a
shoulder, be prepared for a gale of wind. Or
perhaps the birds around the boat were "acting
queer." Strange-acting waterfowl are a bad
omen, a sure warning to "batten down the
hatches." I have yet to develop arthritis, and
in seventeen years of watching birds at sea, I
have never witnessed them doing anything other
than acting like birds. So, fortunately for me,
there are other ways of predicting what weather
lies ahead.

The *Hannah Boden*'s weather fax is like the
fax machines found in business offices, with
the obvious exception of the phone line.
Land-based transmitters send out signals
that are picked up by shipboard receivers
and printed out on fax paper. I am no elec-

tronics genius. To me, it's magic. I turn it on, and it works. The National Oceanic and Atmospheric Administration (NOAA) is responsible for the transmission part of the process, and transmissions include weather analysis maps, twenty-four-hour and thirty-six-hour prognosis maps, sea surface temperature maps, wave height maps, and others. Most important to me are the North Atlantic surface analysis and the sea surface temperature maps.

The surface analysis is a detailed picture of the weather systems for the entire North Atlantic. The map has a grid overlay of latitude and longitude so that I can find my exact location, see what is happening, and predict changes in the weather. The map shows and labels areas of low pressure, high pressure, and frontal systems. Arrows indicate the speed and direction in which these systems are moving, and symbols called "wind flags" represent the speed and direction of the wind in any given area. Isobars, or lines drawn through and connecting areas of similar barometric pressure, are labeled with corresponding pressures so that the ship's barometer may be used to monitor the approach and passage of the different systems seen on the maps. Armed with this information, captains make critical decisions.

The SSB radio is another way to receive weather predictions, and often serves as a second opinion. Even with a detailed analysis map, predicting the future is still very much a game of educated guessing, and some people are better guessers than others. Radio transmissions of a computerized voice are broadcast from various Coast Guard stations; forecasts cover an immense area, from the Caribbean to the eastern portion of the Grand Banks. Both fax maps and SSB broadcasts are often the topics of conversation between fishermen.

The third—and in my opinion, the most accurate—account of the weather is information received from other captains. Weather systems in this part of the world move generally from west to east, making the man west of you your most valuable predictor. What the captain 100 miles to my west is experiencing, I can expect in the very near future.

Every longline fisherman's worst nightmare is to set out a 40-mile string of gear with 1,000 brand-new leaders and wake up to an unexpected gale. It happens. Mother Nature doesn't know about predictions and prognoses, and often defies even the best meteorologists. Stationary highs become mobile and low-pressure systems intensify without warning, resulting in a long and miserable day of hauling gear. The worst scenario is not to get the gear back at all, or to be forced to cut the new leaders from the mainline because of "spin-ups" caused by rough seas. (A spin-up is what we call it when the leaders get tangled around the mainline.) All that time and money gone with just a wink of Mother Nature's eye.

One of the questions I frequently hear from nonfishermen is, if we have all of the high-tech weather equipment and detailed weather information at the tips of our fingers, why would we stay at sea during a hurricane rather than head for the safety of land? It is a good question for which there is a good answer.

Depending upon where I am fishing and how far to the east I end up, the closest point of land might be three days away. St. John's, Newfoundland, would be the port to run for if trying to escape a storm. In order to get to St. John's from the fishing grounds, I would have to steam in a westerly direction, or toward the storm, which is moving from west to east. To get safely ashore and avoid running directly into the storm, I would have to leave the fishing grounds four or even five days before the storm is predicted to be where I am. Is this plausible? No.

Generally, when hurricanes are in a position to be considered four days from the eastern portion of the Grand Banks, they are south of Bermuda and very much undecided about what course they will take. When south of Bermuda, low-pressure systems often act in a whimsical fashion, intensifying, diminishing, and changing direction all of a sudden. By the time a hurricane gets its act together, deciding to steamroll to the northeast, and I am relatively certain that I will be in its path, it is too late to run. The Grand Banks season, June through October, is commonly known as hurricane season. If I'm going to run to the dock every time there is a potential weather threat four days from me, I might as well not leave the dock for the entire five months. Fortunately, many of these low-pressure systems fizzle out or go ashore before they reach the fishing grounds. I have always found it disconcerting to hear a TV weatherman say "...and the storm went safely out to sea."

Preparing a boat for the inevitable and practicing good seamanship are what distinguishes the truly good captains. There are a number of things that I do in preparation for severe weather, and very few things that can be done when in the midst of an ocean storm. Once I have determined that a hurricane is unavoidable, I make a list of things for the crew and myself to do to make the boat as stable as we can and to keep ourselves as safe as possible. My typical list would include the following:

1. Stow all gear that might be blown, torn, or washed from the deck

2. Secure all hatches, doors, and portholes

3. Transfer fuel and fresh water

4. Insure that the boat is on an even keel

5. Check all fuel filters; have spares handy

6. Get away from the Gulf Stream

The stowing of all gear is common sense. It would be discouraging to weather successfully a major storm and have to return to Gloucester without finishing the fishing trip because all of the gear had been washed overboard. And few things would be worse than having a wad of mile-long monofilament fishing line blown from the deck and sucked into the propeller, rendering us helpless and at the mercy of the seas. Without propulsion, the *Hannah Boden* would be tossed around like the wad of mono. Heavy equipment that is bolted through the deck could be ripped from the steel by crashing seas and washed around, damaging itself and anything into which the water sends it smashing. The *Hannah Boden* has a large compartment below the main deck called the "after fish hold," which is perfect for stowing anything that could possibly cause a problem.

Watertight hatches, doors, and portholes are standard equipment aboard fishing boats, but they must be secured properly to insure that they will be effective in keeping water out of the areas they are designed to protect. There is not much scarier than driving a boat through a wicked ocean storm and having "high water" alarms ringing for various compartments. If an alarm goes off indicating high water in the lazarette, the aftermost compartment in the *Hannah Boden*, there is just no way that I can send a man out and across the length of the deck to secure the hatch cover while giant green waves are crashing aboard. In extreme sea conditions, if a man

110

was to be washed overboard, that is probably where he would die.

Transferring fuel and fresh water is done to make tanks as full or as empty as they can be. These liquids are transferred from tank to tank with an electric pump; this is done to minimize something called "free surface effect," or the sloshing back and forth of large quantities of liquid, which can exaggerate the rolling motion of the boat. An alert captain will not be caught with 5,000 gallons of diesel fuel in a 10,000-gallon tank. The *Hannah Boden*'s fuel capacity is almost 20,000 gallons. At approximately 7 pounds per gallon, that would be 140,000 pounds of fuel to slosh around at will if free space is left available to it.

Keeping the boat on an even keel by evenly distributing weight to either side is the most basic seamanship. If a boat is heavier on one side, it is said to have a list. Even the smallest degree of list can be dangerous when magnified by a rolling sea. A list is my personal pet peeve, and attention must be paid to the distribution of ice, fish, fuel, freight, and fresh water, the amounts of each of which are constantly changing during a trip, to maximize stability and to minimize the possibility of rolling completely over in the most extreme situations.

To check the main engine's fuel filters and replace them with new ones if needed is a lesson I learned the hard way. The continual pounding of a boat being driven into a fierce sea acts to loosen the crud that gathers in the bottoms of fuel tanks. The crud mixes with the fuel and is sucked through the fuel lines and into the filters. If enough crud accumulates in the filters it will restrict the flow of fuel to the engine, and once the engine is starved of fuel it dies. The boat is again at the mercy of Mother Nature, and the captain has lost his best defense, his limited control of the boat's motion in a relentless sea. Changing filters and bleeding fuel injectors to get the engine started again are quite the tasks when you are struggling to stand up.

Putting as many miles as I can between the Gulf Stream and myself before the weather reaches a critical stage might minimize the thrashing we will take during the storm, and can be done while most of the other precautions are being completed. The areas, or "pieces of water," where I find the fishing the most productive are where the Gulf Stream pushes up to the north and against the colder water of the Labrador Current. This edge is where I want to set my gear. The Gulf Stream, or "warm side," often has over 3 knots of tide or current, which, when coupled with high wind speeds, helps to agitate the surface of the water and sometimes causes what we refer to as a "confused sea." The sea generally runs in the direction of the wind, and the waves seem to come in sets. When the sea is in a confused state, the waves come from different directions with no particular pattern, and in extreme weather, this complicates seamanship. Also, the hot water of the Gulf Stream tends to give a low-pressure system an added punch. Systems following the hot water seem to thrive. Once the storm is imminent, I steam the boat on a northerly heading, into the colder water and as far away from the Gulf Stream as I can get.

Gathering weather maps, forecasts, and ship reports is part of the daily routine aboard offshore fishing boats. Grand Banks trips are long and exhausting, and no one wants to miss more days of fishing than is absolutely necessary. Bad judgment calls can work both ways. Fishermen are often caught hauling gear in dangerous conditions, and do occasionally secure for weather that never materializes, prolonging the trip another twenty-four hours. Although some of the most successful swordfishing captains are good at playing chicken with Mother Nature and going with their gut feelings, all captains find comfort in a rising barometer and the sound of the stylus scratching across the paper of the fax machine. In addition, I still watch the birds. And if I ever see one doing the backstroke, I'll know all hell is about to break loose.

7

SEA
TIME

Peter had first watch our second night of traveling east, and relieved me at ten o'clock sharp. I was surprised when he reported that he had filled completely the first box of leaders. The short spurt of bad weather might have delayed our progress over the ocean's bottom, but the gear work was still on schedule. I stepped out the back door of the wheel-house and walked around to the bow for a breath of fresh air before turning in. The sky was beautiful, and so clear that the stars appeared close enough to touch. Nights are breathtaking at sea in crystal clear condi-tions, the absence of smog and man-made light allowing the stars and moon their glory. A sliver of the moon, like a crooked smile, lay down low on the horizon, as ready for bed as I was. The moon, like myself, would be spending more time awake at night as our trip progressed. By mid-trip and full moon, at this time of night the moon would be at its peak in the sky, not retiring below the horizon until the wee hours of the next morning.

Leaning against the front of the wheelhouse, the cool of the white steel bulkhead came quickly through my shirt, to rest in the small of my back and my shoulder blades. I shivered, and this was followed by a yawn brought on by the thought of the inevitable sleep deprivation that would begin when the first hooks were cast into the water and would not end until they were wound back aboard for the final time of the trip, possibly three weeks from now. In a very few days, the catching of fish would begin, transporting our internal clocks into some faraway and wacky time zone.

While steaming, the passage of time is measured in distance rather than hours, miles being more powerful than so many sweeps of the second hand. And with the exception of standing watches, the crew and myself are seldom aware of the time of day. An experienced crew member never asks "When will we be there?" but instead might inquire "How many more miles?" At sea, I am almost never cognizant of what day of the week it is, but am keenly aware of how many days must pass to bring the next full moon, the concept of time twisting to meet what is meaningful.

Once we reach the fishing grounds, and the first set is made, the measure against which to mark the passage of time shifts from distance to the number of sets made and pounds of fish onboard. Fishing days are not marked

115

with a conventional clock; eight P.M. has no significance. Dusk is the time to start setting out, and daylight is the time to begin hauling back. Anything between dusk and dawn can be described by the number of sections of gear in or out, whichever applies. Crew members rarely, if ever, wear wristwatches. The clock in the wheelhouse suffices for watch-standing purposes and for the necessary communications with those outside our world of *Hannah Boden* time. I need to know only when ten A.M. rolls around, so I can participate in the fleet's daily radio reports. After ten o'clock, twenty-three other hours may pass, never being acknowledged by name.

I returned to the wheelhouse, wished Peter good-night, and crawled into my bunk, where I slept soundly until Carl woke me at daylight the following morning. We had averaged 9 knots for the past twelve hours, and were now at 43 degrees 24 minutes north and 62 degrees 12 minutes west. I ran below, checked the engine room, and returned to the bridge after stopping in the galley to pour a cup of coffee. The sun was well over the horizon and shone blindingly into the wheelhouse windows, its heat warming my face and chest as I squinted into the white glare. Every twenty-four hours steaming, we gained 5 degrees of longitude to the east, and every 15 degrees of longitude marks a one-hour difference in the time of sunrises and sunsets. At our present position, we saw the sun rise forty minutes before

Gloucester Harbor would, and tomorrow the time gap would reach a full hour. The boats fishing farthest to the east see the sun come up well before the four A.M. mark. Newfoundland is actually in a different time zone than the eastern United States, but because it doesn't matter, we never bother to change the clock back and forth.

Day three was uneventful, which was nice. The crew plugged away at the gear work, enjoying calm seas and sunshine, while I made the slammer baits for the trip. The busywork of preparing the gear for the trip would occupy the crew for the next couple of days and would, we hoped, take us to our first set. Once the gear is in order, the crew find themselves with idle time, which leads to boredom, and boredom sometimes breeds discontent. I have often been amazed with what idle time and the wandering minds of fishermen can come up with, and the desire not to be amazed this trip would soon put pressure on me to get the fishing under way, if for no other reason than to keep the crew busy.

By the time the sun was going down, we were steaming south of Sable Island and the second box of leaders was full. Sable Island is a narrow and low strip of land inhabited by wild horses and the ghosts of men lost at sea in this area, called "the graveyard of the North Atlantic." The dangerous areas of shallow water surrounding Sable Island have claimed more ships than has the Bermuda Triangle, and since the *Hannah Boden*'s sister ship, the *Andrea Gail*, went down in this vicinity in the Halloween gale of 1991, I have been spooked every trip while passing by.

I sat now and thought back to steaming home to Gloucester on that trip from which the *Andrea Gail* never returned. As we approached the Sable Island area from the east, bound for home, Bob Brown asked that we pass the island closer and slower than usual, taking time to look for some sign of the *Andrea Gail*. She was one week overdue in her homecoming, and the Canadian Coast Guard had found evidence that she might have experienced some trouble in the area surrounding Sable Island. There wasn't a breath of wind that day, and the fog was so thick it collected in cold drops that clung to our eyebrows and lashes. We couldn't see 100 feet from the boat. But still we looked. We searched in the fog all day, hoping to stumble into the scene that played on the reel-to-reel in my head. My mind's eye saw a raft, which, when we got closer, we could see held the six fishermen from the *Andrea Gail*, all smiling and waving.

Like a mirage in a desert, the fog can play tricks with your eyes and mind, showing you whatever you want to see if you look hard enough. We had been squinting into the fog over the bow for hours when something white appeared in the water ahead of us. It didn't disappear when I blinked. It was real. A plastic 55-gallon drum loomed eerily through the vapor. As we neared it, I maneuvered the boat so that the barrel floated slowly down the starboard rail, where the crew pulled it aboard. It was marked clearly with the letters "A.G.," and was not what I had hoped to find. The presence of the barrel from the *Andrea Gail* on our deck brought with it feelings of doom and hopelessness, and I was tempted to throw it back overboard.

The Coast Guard had canceled its search by the time we arrived in Gloucester three days later, and by then any shred of hope that anyone still clung to rested with my crew and myself. We had no good news for the families and friends of the men lost with the *Andrea Gail*. In fact, we had only the empty barrel, a small piece of the puzzle. We didn't know anything that the Coast Guard hadn't already reported, and could give nobody reason to deny the fact that the boat and her six-man crew were gone forever.

Now it was dark, and the *Hannah Boden* slid silently through the water 17 miles south of Sable Island, a ridiculously wide distance to pass the shoals safely, but not quite enough to stop the goose bumps from creeping up my back and racing up and down my arms. The breeze made haunting sounds through the *Hannah Boden*'s rigging, like someone blowing across the opening of a Coke bottle, causing the hairs on the back of my neck to prickle. I had never seen a ghost, and knew that my imagination was working overtime, but I didn't feel calm until I could no longer see Sable Island on the radar screen. At this point it didn't matter if ghosts existed in reality or not; they certainly would not follow us all the way to the Grand Banks. Staring into the emptiness of the blank radar screen, I hoped that our return to Gloucester would take us by Sable Island in the light of day.

The next morning, big, white, cumulus clouds drifted eastward, selfishly interrupting the sun's light, which had traveled so far to warm the decks of the *Hannah Boden*. But the sun was persistent and broke through holes in the clouds, resulting in vertical columns of multicolored light that landed in bright yellow splotches in the sea around us. The columns of light were so definite, their edges so distinct, I was tempted to steer the boat around them to avoid crashing into and toppling them. The water around the splotches that supported the columns was dark blue. I stood on the bow and gazed down into the ocean. Shaded by the clouds, the water below my feet was the color of a metal pail full of Isle Au Haut blueberries. A bit of sun sneaked through the clouds above and hit me on the back of the head, casting my shadow onto the sea. With the sunlight, the berries vanished, and the ocean took on a greenish tint, characteristic of cold water, as opposed to the light and sparkly blue color the sun picks out of the warmer Gulf Stream or the Caribbean.

"What do you think, Ma?" Carl's voice

startled me, and I turned aft toward the front of the wheelhouse.

"I think it looks green," I said, referring to the color of the water, which is a common topic of conversation aboard a swordboat. The water's color often indicates what might be caught in it when fished. "What do you think?"

Carl leaned over the handrail that followed the deck around the bow, exposing a tan line at his T-shirt collar. After a thorough examination of the water below, Carl spoke with the thick Maine accent that reminded me of home. "Yup. It looks sharky to me. How many miles to go before we set?"

"At least three hundred, maybe four or five. It depends on how much poking around I have to do to get situated and how far to the east we have to go to get clear of the other boats."

Carl pulled his Marlboros from his shirt pocket and lit one up. He spoke now with the end of the cigarette wagging up and down as if hinged with a swivel to his lower lip. "We should have all the gear work done by tomorrow. I'm finishing up the ball-drops today. We're stopping for a sandwich now. Do you want anything?"

"No thanks, Carl. I'll get something later." As he walked away from me, I called after him. "Hey, have you and Peter kissed and made up yet?" Carl stopped and turned back toward me. He cocked his head to the side, raised one dark eyebrow, and, without moving another muscle, threw daggers from his deep black pupils that landed in the bull's-eye around my heart. He never said another word; he didn't have to. He took a thoughtful drag from his cigarette, shook his head, and turned again to leave. "Jesus, sorry I asked." And I was. I considered this strike two in as many attempts to guide Carl into curbing his behavior with regard to race relations, and not wanting to strike out, I decided to sit on the bench for a while. "I guess I won't bring that up again," I said to myself, and headed for the wheelhouse door.

As I stepped through the door Charlie was just coming up the stairs, his beard a bit less shaggy than it had been the day we threw the lines. "Hi, Charlie! Where have you been hiding? I haven't laid eyes on you since we left the dock." This was Charlie's third trip with me, and I was quite fond of him. He had a pleasant disposition and a good work ethic. I sensed in Charlie maturity and fairness, and hoped that when and if the battle lines were drawn between Carl and Peter, Charlie, like Ringo, would be wise enough to help keep the situation from getting out of hand.

"Hello, Captain. I've been laying low. I haven't felt right for three days. Seasick, I guess."

"Seasick? No, you've never been seasick before. It's probably a flu."

"Yeah, you're right. My youngest daughter was sick when we were home. I must have caught whatever she had." Other than Peter, the only family man among the crew, Charlie often spoke of his girls while at sea, and obviously missed them deeply. "Do you have any Pepto-Bismol or Alka-Seltzer?"

"Sorry, I don't. Have you been eating?" I asked, and remembered that I had noticed that Charlie didn't look good the morning we left Gloucester, and now he appeared even thinner than usual.

"It hasn't affected my appetite. I hope I feel better by the time we start fishing."

"Me, too. Get plenty of sleep while you can."

"I will. See you later." Charlie left me sitting in the chair and wondering if I should be worried about his health. I suspected, and later realized, that whatever the ailment was, Pepto-Bismol would not be the cure. A familiar voice through the static of the SSB radio beckoned me from my concern for Charlie for the time being. Larry Thompson, captain and owner of the *Sea Lion VIII*, was calling me.

I knew that Larry must have been nearing the end of his trip because he had made several sets before I left the grounds on my previous trip. I answered him, "Whiskey Romeo Charlie five two four five. Hello, L.T. What's happening? Over."

"Hi, Linda. Are you on your way back out yet? Over."

"Roger. Forty-four oh eight north and fifty-four forty-one west. We'll be there in a couple of days. Over."

"Jesus. You didn't waste much time at the dock...two days? Over."

"Roger, L.T. We're really trying to stay on the moon. How's the fishing? Over."

"Bad. It's been slow since you left. We're hoping it will pick up on the first quarter. I've only got a handful of sets left to make, but I guess we'll squeak a trip out of it. We're grinding away on fifteen hundred pounds a night, nothing special. How's your weather? Over."

"The weather's beautiful. Light westerly. What's your position? Over."

"We're like...forty-three north and forty-seven west. I'm about in the middle of the pack as far as the lineup goes. The *Northern Venture* and the *Eagle Eye* are fishing on a strip up to the northeast and are doing a little better than the rest of us, but it's too late in the trip for me to move farther from the dock. Over."

"Right. Is the hot water backing off yet? Over."

"No, not yet. Okay, Linda, I have to get ready to set out. Thanks for the weather report. Check you tomorrow. Whiskey Uniform Victor six zero niner eight. Clear."

"Thanks for the check. Good luck with it tonight. Whiskey Romeo Charlie five two four five. 'Bye."

I now had a better idea of where the fleet was located, and marked Larry's position on the chart. About 150 miles west of where I had fished last trip, Larry's position was only four berths away from where I wanted to be. If the *Sea Lion VIII* was in the middle of a string of fifteen or twenty boats, there was no way that I could possibly squeeze into my favorite corner. I was close enough to the fleet to

124

hear most of the SSB conversation, and would start writing down positions, water temperatures, number of remaining sets, and number of fish caught to form a strategy of where I might find a productive berth. As I strained to pick up details through the ever-present static of the SSB, I watched out the back windows as Carl filled the ball-drop spool.

It was dusk. Carl worked at the starboard rail making ball-drops and winding them onto an aluminum spool with a hand crank. Ball-drops are pieces of 250-pound-test monofilament, usually a different color than what is used for leaders, with a snap on one end and a loop tied into the other. When the gear is set out, a bullet float is secured to the loop end and the snap goes onto the mainline, just like a leader. The floats prevent the gear from sinking to the bottom, and the drops are cut to length to allow the hooks to hang at whatever depth the captain thinks will be optimal for catching the most fish. On the Grand Banks, I use 5-fathom drops, allowing the mainline to sink to 30 feet below the surface. With 7-fathom leaders, the baited hooks hang at 12 fathoms, or 72 feet. Even 72 feet is considered relatively shallow given that the depth of water in which we usually fish is over 3,000 fathoms, leaving 31/2 miles of salt water between the bottom of the boat and the ocean floor.

Carl worked quickly, with an economy of motion. As the circumference of the gear on the spool neared its maximum capacity, I wondered what more I could find for Carl to do to keep his mind on business and off harassing Peter for the next few days. Once fish started coming aboard, the problem would take care of itself. Carl would be too busy working even to throw Peter a dirty look.

Another night, another day, and another 200 miles of the North Atlantic passed beneath the keel of the *Hannah Boden*. Again I hung the SSB's mike back into its bracket after a conversation with Larry T. similar to the one the night before: reports of fair weather from me and poor fishing from the fleet. I had monitored the radio all day, and had drawn a diagram of the lineup of the sixteen U.S. swordboats that were presently fishing. It was discouraging to have traveled all this distance and learn that no great amount of fish was being caught. It was decision time for me, and I opted to change course to the north a few degrees and steam past the bulk of the fleet to join the *Northern Venture* and the *Eagle Eye*, who had left the fleet in search of better fishing. It is always best to search, or "scope out," at the beginning of the trip and try to find a spot that will produce fish every night for the duration of the sets needed, rather than to set out prematurely or hastily and have to pick up and move again.

It was six-thirty on our fifth night at sea. We were just crossing the Canadian line on the east side of the "tail of the bank" and were about to enter international water. I turned the autopilot to subtract 14 degrees from our course for a heading of 85° compass that would bring us to our new destination of 46° 20' N and 43° 30' W in twenty-nine hours at our present speed of 9.6 knots. There was always the chance that we could run into a piece of water before reaching our destination, and once in international water, anything is fair game, but if the latest fax was accurate, we would have to steam every one of the 280 miles that lay between our present position and our ultimate destination.

Tonight the crew would record the surface water temperature and our position every thirty minutes. On the watch bill would be instructions to wake me if the temperature should rise above 65 degrees Fahrenheit. The surface temperature gauge consists of a transducer on the bottom of the hull connected by a wire to the readout in the wheelhouse. The readout displays the temperature of the water directly under the boat, in red numbers, in hundredths of degrees. The surface temperature was 56.00, and I entered it in the table that I had drawn in my notebook, along with our position and the time.

Charlie had the first watch and entered the wheelhouse a few minutes before ten P.M. If he felt as bad as he looked, he was suffering terribly. I inquired about how he was feeling, and could tell he was lying when he said "Better." Better than what? I wondered. Charlie's complexion was washed out, and it appeared he had to muster all of his strength to climb into the chair. Charlie's beard was showing more gray than I had noticed before, and his hair looked like it had spent many hours mashed against a pillow.

"Will we be fishing tomorrow night?" he asked.

"I doubt it. The reports from the fleet haven't been very good. We might as well try somewhere they aren't."

"Sounds good to me. I could sure use another day to kick this flu."

"Okay, here's the watch bill," I said as I handed him the notebook. "I need for you to record water temp. Have a good night, and I'll see you in the morning."

I didn't sleep well that night. My mind was feeling the first of the pressure to get located on a piece of water and begin fishing, and I was worried that Charlie's flu might linger. The crew was done with the gear work; they were ready to fish. They could only watch movies and play cards for so long....

Ringo woke me at daylight with a cheerful, "Good morning, Ma. Time to find the mother lode."

"Thanks, Tom. I'll be right out," I answered through the door. When I entered the wheelhouse, Ringo was filling in the last blank line on the watch bill; his mop of blond hair, which hadn't seen the inside of his baseball cap all night, was on the wild side. I glanced up at the red numbers on the face of the temperature gauge. "Brrr...fifty-seven degrees. I guess we're not quite there yet."

Ringo handed me the notebook. "That's tropical compared to what it's been all night. We must be getting close. Do you think we'll set tonight? We're ready."

"I want to get east of the *Eagle Eye* and the *Northern Venture*, and that won't be until late tonight, so don't get the bait out yet. I know you're all anxious."

"All of us but Charlie. He's quite sick. Carl's taking bets on whether he'll last the trip or not."

"Has Dr. Carl ruled out the flu?"

"Yes, he has. The doctor has concluded that if it were the flu, we would all have it by now...such close quarters. I have to agree."

"Oh, great, a second opinion. How's the Carl-and-Peter thing?"

"Carl sprayed an entire can of Right Guard into Peter's stateroom and covered his walls with those stick-on air fresheners. Peter pretended to not notice, so I guess everything is just fine."

"That little bastard! I asked him—"

"You asked him to stop with the name-calling, which he has. You know what the problem is, Ma?"

"No. Please tell me."

"The problem is that we haven't had a green guy to torment all summer, no whipping post. Jesus, Carl is even getting on *me*."

"How so?"

"He greets me every morning with 'Hey, old fuck! Don't forget to take your Geritol.' Peter and I are conspiring to suffocate him in his bunk and credit the loss to Sudden Infant Death."

129

At this I had to laugh. "I didn't realize that having such an experienced crew would be this much trouble. I'll have to hire green guys to fill the positions vacated by Carl and Charlie."

Ringo headed below, saying that he would check the engine room and put on a pot of coffee for me. I began to think about the absence of a green guy. I usually enjoyed having a totally inexperienced man aboard for a trip. The new guy is generally young, excited about and interested in all that goes on. Of course, there is a certain initiation process that takes place, a mild form of hazing that occurs. Practical jokes and lighthearted teasing are most often the extent of the ritual and seldom get out of hand. Most frequently, the practical jokes occur during idle time, born of the boredom with steaming for several days or prolonged periods of poor fishing.

I remembered the most fun we ever had with a green guy, a big, dumb kid whom we affectionately called "Jethro." Jethro was from a small town in Maine, and his first trip offshore was also his first time away from home. Jethro's initiation started with the usual and harmless "mail buoy" prank. The gang told Jethro of a fictitious buoy that was owned and operated by the U.S. Postal Service and anchored in the middle of the Grand Banks. Jethro was easily convinced that he could deposit letters in the buoy to be delivered to his family and friends informing them of his adventures at sea. Jethro's evenings were spent composing letters, asking for and receiving spelling help from his shipmates. When we were approaching the alleged buoy, Jethro was found to have no postage stamps, so he was informed that he could not send his mail. He was disappointed, but understood that the postman can't deliver unstamped letters. He would know better the next time.

Jethro made countless trips to the engine room and wheelhouse, looking for things that do not exist. The crew sent him up to the bridge one afternoon to retrieve the "chain stretcher," for which he searched with diligence. After he had totally emptied every storage cupboard of its contents, I asked him what the hell he was looking for. He answered, "The chain stretcher," and resumed his search. I asked if he knew what a chain stretcher looked like, and he answered, "No, but I think I'll recognize it when I see it." To this day I haven't figured out how someone can search for an item without the slightest clue what it might look like; although Jethro was determined, he never found the chain stretcher.

To me, the truest testimony to Jethro's IQ is the joke that Ringo set up to see just how gullible Jethro could be. Next to the water fountain in the wheelhouse, Ringo placed an empty 1-gallon plastic milk jug on which he had written in black marker "DEHYDRATED H_2O." Apparently, Jethro had been complaining about drinking soda, and wished he had some other beverage. Not long after the jug had been left in the wheelhouse, up came Jethro, scouting around again. "What are you doing up here? Don't you have work to do on deck?" I snapped at him.

"Well, I'm thirsty, and Ringo said that there might be some dehydrated H-two-O up here."

"Oh, yeah. It's right there," I said, and pointed to the milk jug.

Jethro held up the jug and read the lettering: "Dee-hi-drated-H-two-O. This is it. Ringo says all I have to do is add water to it and I'll have a very refreshing drink."

"Well, Ringo's right. Make sure you shake it up good before you drink it."

"Okay, thanks." Jethro filled the jug with ice-cold water from the fountain and shook it vigorously as he made his way back down the stairs. I asked him later how he liked the drink, and he said that it was quite good and he hoped we had more.

Once Jethro had consumed several gallons of the water, phase two of the plan kicked in. At night, when the crew was done work and taking off their oil gear, they sat and inspected their bare feet, looking for signs of "yellow foot." They explained to Jethro that yellow foot was a painful disease that had many causes, one of which was wearing rubber boots for prolonged periods, another was not properly shaking the dehydrated water before consumption. Jethro soon joined the others in the foot examination, seemingly relieved not to have contracted the affliction that could, if left untreated, result in the amputation of toes.

When Jethro had reached the proper level of concern, Carl dumped poultry seasoning into Jethro's boots one night while we slept. The following day was a particularly long and hot one. Everyone's feet sweltered in the black rubber boots. I smelled something similar to roasted turkey long before any boots were kicked off for the night, but Jethro didn't seem to notice anything peculiar until he yanked off his right boot at about midnight. The foot of his tube sock was stained bright yellow. His eyes opened wide and his jaw dropped. He pulled off the left boot with such fury that the sock flew off with it, exposing a foot yellow up to the ankle. "I've got it," he muttered.

"Jesus, Jethro. That's the worst case I've ever seen. Take off your right sock and let's have a look." Ringo feigned intense concern.

Jethro painstakingly and gently pulled at the other sock, appearing to be afraid to touch it, as if the disease might spread to his hands. We all stood over him and watched as he inched the top of the elastic tube down over his foot and finally off. The five of us joined Jethro in a choral gasp of horror as we viewed the sickly-looking feet. The toes, balls, and heels of both feet were the darkest, a brownish yellow. The arches and insteps were the hue of French's mustard, and as the color neared the ankle areas, it faded to the pallor of an old bruise. "Does it hurt?" I asked.

"Not yet, but it sure stinks. What can I do now? I can't work like this. Do we have any medicine? I think I should see a doctor. Will you take me in?"

Before I could answer in the negative, Carl jumped in. "No way! We ain't goin' in till the fish hold is full. She told us that before we left the dock."

"That's right," Kenny chimed in. "I don't care if every last fuckin' toe rots and falls off. It's his own fault, Ma. We warned him to shake that shit up before drinking it."

"I agree," Ringo added. "It's your own fault, Jethro. Why should we all suffer because of you? Besides, the worst that can happen is you'll lose your toes. You aren't going to die or anything. What's the big deal?"

"I don't want to lose my toes. Isn't there anything I can do to save them?" Jethro was starting to sound quite desperate, and when he looked up at me, I could see a tear forming in his eye.

I thought the joke had gone just about as far as it could, and not wanting a basket case on my hands, or for Jethro to humiliate himself by crying in front of the crew, I had a revelation. "Hey! I have an idea. Yellow foot starts on the outside and works its way through the skin and eventually to the bones, which is when the pain starts. There's a good chance that the infection hasn't completely penetrated the skin yet. Why don't you try taking a hot shower? Really scrub those feet."

"Do you think it will work?"

"Well, it won't do any harm. You're not in pain, so the infection can't be very deep."

Ringo finally came to my rescue. "There's some hydrogen peroxide in the medicine chest above the washing machine. Dump some on both feet after you wash them."

Jethro hobbled off toward the crew's head, being careful not to bend his toes as he walked. The rest of the crew and I enjoyed a bowl of ice cream while we waited anxiously around the galley table for the results of the antidote. Jethro emerged from the head in a cloud of steam that smelled like hot chicken soup. His feet showed not a trace of yellow, but were quite red from the scouring they had received. "I think it worked!" Jethro was jubilant. I said my good-nights to them all and asked Jethro to throw his contaminated boots and socks overboard. As I climbed the stairs to go to bed, I heard Carl offer to "rent" Jethro a pair of boots for the rest of the trip. There has never been a recurrence of yellow foot aboard the *Hannah Boden*, and Jethro was content to drink soda until we returned to Gloucester two weeks later.

"Maybe Ringo's right. Maybe we do need a new guy to play with," I said to myself. "Too late for this trip." I found our position on the chart, 45 degrees 15 minutes north and 46 degrees 52 minutes west, twelve hours from where David, on the *Northern Venture*, had started his set last night. By dinnertime we would be in the area where David and John, the captain of the *Eagle Eye*, were fishing, allowing me nearly twenty-four hours to scope out the water and get in a position to set out the gear the following night.

I sat and stared at the temperature gauge all day, leaving the chair only to check the engine room and to talk with my fellow fishermen on the radio. By early evening I was 2 miles north of the *Northern Venture* and the warm strip of water on which he and John had been fishing. John was 40 miles to our east and setting toward David, who was setting to the west also.

"Looks like we've got company, John," I heard David say on channel 9 of the VHF radio.

"Oh, yeah? Who's that?" John asked.

"I don't know, but I can see running lights, and I have a target two miles north of me on the radar. Over."

I picked up the VHF mike and broke into the conversation. "It's Linda on the *Hannah Boden*. I'm going to get east of John to set tomorrow night. Over."

"Hi, Linda! Hey, John, it's the girl with the big green boat. She's steaming for the slot east of you," David said.

"Oh, okay, ask her to put her radio up on high power so I can hear her," John replied.

I did so and called John. "Hello, John. Can you hear me now? Over."

"Roger. Hi, Linda. Are you just getting out? Over."

"Roger. We haven't set yet. I guess we'll get started tomorrow night. I'm in the cold water

136

above your strip and will stay here until I get around your eastern end so I don't part either of you off with the birds. Over."

"Yeah, that's good. Let's see, you're coming toward me...I should see you on radar in a couple of hours. I'm not getting any cooler than sixty-one, so if you'll stay north of that, we'll be fine. My east end beeper is one-six-seven-six. It's a good strong one, so you shouldn't have any trouble finding it. Over."

I scribbled "1676—John's east end" in my notebook. "Okay, John. Thanks for that. I'll let you pay attention to your set, and I'll be listening for fish reports tomorrow. Over."

"Roger. I hope we can give you some good news. It's been pretty good here for the last five sets, like thirty fish a night, hundred-pound average. The strip is getting a bit narrower each set, and there's not much current, but the fishing has been steady. Over."

"That sounds all right. Thanks again for the info. Good luck to you both, and good night. 'Bye." I placed the mike in its bracket and reached up to turn on the RDF. I tuned the RDF to 1676 and waited to hear John's beeper; the transmissions are on a timer, going off for fifteen seconds every few minutes, prolonging the life of the 18-volt battery. When the beeper sounded its Morse code series of beeps, I heard them through the RDF's speaker, but it was not a strong enough signal for the needle to respond with a point in any direction. I was at least 40 miles from the beeper, so I turned the volume of the RDF down and returned to the chair, where I resumed my watch on the temperature gauge. I would check John's beeper again in an hour or so, and in the meantime would steer the *Hannah Boden* in an easterly direction, staying in 56- to 58-degree water. David's boat was now west of me and his gear to my south, running east and west in the warmest part of the strip, which I had been told was 67 degrees. As I steamed I got into 60-degree water and knew I was getting too close to where David's gear was, so to get back into the cooler water, I steered a few degrees to port. Captains get quite upset and often irate when another boat steams across their gear with stabilizing birds in the water. The birds catch the mainline, dragging it through the water until it parts off. Chasing bitter ends while hauling back consumes valuable time and is most frustrating when necessitated by the carelessness of another fisherman.

As I settled back into the chair, Charlie came up the stairs with my dinner. "Hello, my name is Pierre, and I will be your waiter this evening." Charlie bowed slightly at the waist and handed me a plate of prime rib, baked potato, and fresh asparagus. He pulled a can of diet Pepsi from his back pocket and cradled it in both hands, holding it out for my inspection. "I believe this is what you ordered, Madam." I nodded my approval. "An excellent choice with the beef," he said.

Charlie popped the top of the can open to "let it breathe" and set it on the console. "Now, if there is anything else you will be needing, please beat vigorously upon the floor with a large hammer. Bon appetit." Although still pale, and thinner than normal, Charlie had regained his smile and the twinkle in his eyes. He must, I thought, be feeling better.

My server neglected to bring me a knife with which to cut my meat. I found my deck knife and pulled it from its sheath. The blade was well rusted, and there was a wad of crud crusted up around the wooden handle, probably dried blood and fish slime. I couldn't bring myself to use the smelly thing on my meal, and having no large hammer in my possession, set my plate in the chair and went below for a steak knife.

Four of the men sat around the galley table eating and talking over the usual background of *Lonesome Dove*. I opened a drawer and pulled out a steak knife. "Where's my waiter?" I asked, and was told that Charlie had gone to his bunk, where he had spent most of the day. He didn't feel like eating, so Ringo had wrapped his meal in tinfoil and stuck it in the refrigerator for Charlie to eat later. Apparently, Charlie had made it clear that he didn't want to worry me. "Gee, I thought he was feeling better. He looks better, don't you think?" I asked the group.

The men stared at one another in silence. Finally, Carl spoke up. "He don't look too fuckin' healthy to me. For twenty bucks you can join the pool. Whoever guesses closest to Charlie's expiration date wins the pot. I've got September fifteenth, Kenny's got the twenty-second, and Ringo is optimistic with October first. Peter don't wanna play."

"Neither do I," I said, and returned to the wheelhouse. I denied myself the natural reaction of being upset about Carl's pool. "We've got to get fishing. These guys have too much free time on their hands," I mumbled as I sat, placing the plate of food in my lap. The crew would gamble and have pools on everything and anything when battling boredom. Usually, cigarettes and dishwashing duties were what was at stake. The losers get dishpan hands, and the winners lung cancer. A poker game is not out of the ordinary for the steam home, but I always discourage the men from playing for money, as it can cause problems. Toothpicks and candy bars make good poker chips and don't raise emotions the way paychecks do.

We once had a government observer who worked for the National Marine Fisheries Service aboard for a trip. A polite young man, Luke was well liked by the crew and myself. While steaming home from the trip, Luke joined Peter and Carl in a poker game despite my friendly advice not to do so. In less than an hour Peter had taken Luke for every dime he had in his possession and most of what he had coming for his days at sea. Carl ended up with Luke's wristwatch, which he wore with pride until returning it to Luke at the dock, claiming to have no use for it. Unfortunately for Luke, Peter did have a use for his money.

I ate my meal while staring at the temperature gauge and making small adjustments to the autopilot to keep the boat in the 56-to-58-degree range. I took my plate and silverware below to be washed. Kenny stood at the sink with his arms in soapy water up to his elbows. "Place them right here on the counter, Ma," Kenny said.

"I'm up first tonight. What time do you want to start watches?" Ringo asked.

"Probably not until late, if at all. I'm steaming around the *Eagle Eye*'s east end, then I'll start scouting the area. I'll want to get a sense of the temperature below the surface as soon as we're clear of John's gear. I'll get a couple of you up when I'm ready. Oh, and thanks for dinner. It was delicious."

Returning topside, I turned up the volume on the RDF and waited a minute for "1676" to signal. When it started beeping this time, the direction-indicating needle swung from a nine o'clock position to about twelve-thirty, and stayed there until the transmission ceased. Twelve o'clock being straight ahead, John's buoy was just off our heading to the starboard, where I wanted to keep it until we were completely by it. I cranked the radar's range knob up from 12 miles to 24, and saw a small target at 18 miles ahead of us. Thirty minutes later I could see the lights of the *Eagle Eye*, and called John on the VHF.

"Pick me up, John? *Eagle Eye. Hannah Boden.*"

"I see you there at nine miles, Linda. Over."

"I have a bead on your end buoy, how far is it behind you? Over."

"Ah...about twelve miles. Over."

"Okay, I guess I'll be another couple hours catching up with it. How's the set looking tonight? Over."

"About the same. Three nights ago this strip was four miles wide, and tonight it was only two where I started. The warmest water I've seen tonight is sixty-six point five-oh. I had as high as sixty-eight point zero last night. I hope we get a few more sets on it before it totally disappears. Over."

"Yeah. Me too. I need to set out tomorrow night. My crew is getting restless; too much steaming. Over." I hated hearing myself say that setting out was a "need" dictated by the crew rather than a desire we all felt to get busy doing something we enjoyed. And I hoped that I would not sacrifice a berth that might be more productive simply because I wanted to diminish the crew's idle time.

"Roger. You should be fine going from my east end to the east. Well, good luck looking. Talk to you tomorrow. Over."

Shortly after I spoke with John, Bob called on the SSB. I filled him in on what was going on and agreed that we would talk the next night. Bob rarely missed a night of checking on us. It is comforting to know that the boss will call when you have a problem and need his advice on how to solve it or fix something that might have broken. Bob had talked me through many mechanical problems over the radio; he knew intimately every system on the boat. I chose not to share with the boss my concerns over Charlie's health or Carl's hateful behavior toward Peter, believing that both would take care of themselves once there was no time for anything but work.

By ten-thirty P.M., we were finally east of "1676," and I turned the boat hard to starboard to steam across the strip. Heading due south, I watched the surface temperature creep slowly up from 59.00 to 60.50, where it fluctuated up and down three tenths of a degree, from 60.20 to 60.50, for close to a mile. In the next quarter mile the gauge raced to 66.70, where it flattened out, remaining at the same temperature for another quarter mile. Still heading south, the temperature slowly dropped back down to 58.00 over the distance of 2 miles. At this point, I thought the break on the north side of the hottest water had the most potential as it was the "sharpest," meaning it showed the greatest temperature change in the shortest distance. In the area where the temperature went from 60.50 to 66.70 on the north side of the strip is where I would want my gear. But this determination took into account only the surface temperature, which is all I knew so far.

Next I would have to check the current on the surface in different parts of the strip by doing a series of drift tests. In 58-degree water on the south side, the offshore side of the strip, I slowed the boat to an idle and pulled the gearshift back into neutral. I waited as the forward motion of the *Hannah Boden* through the water slowed and eventually stopped. I placed an "event mark" on the plotter marking our present position with a small blue cross and set the bridge alarm for fifteen minutes.

As I waited for the alarm, I turned on the night hauling light that was secured to the starboard outrigger; it shone straight down, directly into the ocean beside the hull. I concentrated on the bright spot in the water for a few minutes, hoping to see the light attract small bait fish or squid to it; no prey, no predators. I switched on the searchlight mounted outside on the wheelhouse roof and worked the directional control handle from my platform in the after section of the bridge. I scanned the bright beam along the surface of the water around us, and also scanned the sky. The water's surface showed no action of jumping bait fish, and the sky held no birds. Switching off the searchlight, I looked again at the lighted water below the hauling station; still nothing, dead water.

The alarm sounded the end of the fifteen-minute drift test. The plotter showed that our position had changed one tenth of a nautical mile in an easterly direction. The current in the 58-degree water south of the strip was about half a knot to the east.

Knocking the boat back into gear, I steamed due north, into the middle of the strip, where I repeated the drift test and light checks in the 66.60-degree water. The fifteen minutes of drifting indicated 1 knot of easterly tide; the lights again found no sign of life in the area. Disappointed but determined, I repeated the routine in 59-degree water north of the strip, again finding nothing to get excited about. "Jesus, these guys are catching fish in a desert." I sighed.

The time had come to try the down temp, so I ran below to get the guys to help me put the down temp bird into the water. Kenny, Ringo, and Carl sat around the galley table. "What are you guys doing up? I figured you would be fast asleep by now."

"Waiting for you, Ma," Kenny said. "Are you ready for the down temp?"

"I sure am."

"How's it looking so far?"

"Not too sporty. No life, and very little tide. But John and David are catching a few fish, so I guess we can."

"We'll kick their asses," Carl said.

"I like your confidence. Let's go!" I left the galley and returned to the wheelhouse, where I looked out the back windows and waited for the men to appear on deck. The yellow fiberglass down temp bird rested in its bracket at the port-side stern quarter of the boat, just inside the rail. The bird is about the same size and shape as the steel stabilizing birds; although it is much lighter, it still requires two men to lift it from its bracket. Attached to the bird is a cable that serves two functions. The cable allows the bird to be towed through the water at different depths, and also supplies a piece of electronics in the wheelhouse with water temperature information and depth in fathoms. The purpose of the down temp is to give the captain a reading of the water's temperature below the surface. I like to tow the bird at 12 fathoms, the same depth at which my hooks will be fishing. Often a break that looks good on the surface has ice water under it, which can be shark infested. Also, flat and uninteresting surface water might be lying over a sharp break that can be detected only with the down temp.

The cable runs from the bird, through a large block that hangs on a short davit mounted on the port stern quarter, and up to a hydraulic winch on the deck behind the wheelhouse. The valve that controls the winch is on the aft console of the bridge in front of where I was standing and looking out the back windows. Carl and Kenny lifted the bird from its bracket and set it on the rail. I pulled the handle that turned the winch, hauling in the slack cable until the bird was raised just slightly from the rail. As the men swung the davit's arm overboard, I put the boat in gear and idled ahead slowly. With the davit locked into place, the bird now hung over the water. I pushed the valve's handle to back the winch off, lowering the bird gently into the water. As the bird dove down, it pulled the cable from the winch. When the gauge indicated that the bird was swimming at 18 fathoms, I turned off the valve and Ringo tightened down the manual brake on the winch. As I pushed the throttle up to 1,500 RPMs, which is our normal setting speed, the depth of the bird came up to 12 fathoms as it was towed through the water.

I yelled "Thanks" to the guys and returned to the front of the wheelhouse, where I could see the plotter, the surface temp, and the down temp gauges, which read 58 on the surface and 58 at 12 fathoms. I steamed south, back across the strip. The surface gauge went up and back down, as it had before, but the down temp never changed. Flat 58-degree water lay beneath the strip. I thought that if I didn't know John and David were catching swordfish, I would never think to set a hook here.

I didn't have a good feeling about this berth—or the fact that I had steamed six days to reach it. But I had until the next afternoon to figure out how to make the most of it. I steamed east for the next five hours, going slowly back and forth across the strip at very small angles, watching the surface temperature go hotter and colder while the down temperature remained steady. When I was 40 miles east of where John had started, I marked the plotter with another cross to represent where we might start our first set. Now going across the strip at a 90-degree angle, from north to south, I noted that the warmest water was only 65.85 and the down temp had also dropped, reading 56. The width of the strip was narrower here, too, another bad sign as far as I was concerned. I wondered whether I should turn the Doppler on and scout around for some positive sign with it. Or whether I should steam away from the strip and hope to find some other piece of water to fish the next night. The strip showed signs of disappearing, but if I decided to go hunting, there was no guarantee that I would find anything better. If I chose to leave the strip, how long would it be before we would start fishing? What kind of trouble could the crew dream up with a few more days of nothing to do but think?

I studied the chart where I had penciled in the rest of the fleet, and thought that there was a possibility that I could steam south and run into the main break well northeast of the easternmost boat, and fish between the fleet and the strip. Although the main break hadn't been producing nearly as much as the strip, that could certainly change as the moon increased. It usually does, and the main break is not apt to evaporate after a few sets, leaving me homeless and hunting again.

At four-thirty A.M. I struggled to make a tough decision: to leave the strip in search of something that I might be able to get excited about, or to stay and get the ball rolling. Leaving it was more of a gamble. If I fished here, I would be pretty sure to catch what the others were catching. If I struck out for a spot that might be more productive, I took the chance that it would be absolutely terrible. I finally decided to take my chances and search for a new location. I set the autopilot on due south, leaving behind the guarantee that we would set out that night. I sat back to watch the gauges for what I knew from experience could be hundreds of agonizing miles, each of which would be closely watched through the eyes of the crew as the numbers crept up and down on the GPS, our shipboard way of watching the clock.

8

MUG-UP

Fishermen, especially those of an earlier vintage, are superstitious; we have a unique set of superstitions by which we live. Some landlubbers will think certain seagoing rituals foolish and consider bizarre our avoidance of seemingly harmless words, actions, and things. However, when the stakes are high and the consequences that threaten severe, even the most rational among us will observe the rituals—just in case they hold merit.

Pork in any shape or form was strictly taboo aboard the *Walter Leeman*, as was merely speaking the word *pig*. Captain Alden actually went so far as to forbid me from thinking the word, an order I unsuccessfully tried to follow. The pig thing is perhaps the foremost superstition among fishermen. Pigs and water just don't jive. I have heard two differing opinions on why pigs are taboo, both of which seem logical to me. One is that pigs can't swim; they roll over onto their backs and drown. The other is that pigs do indeed swim, but while doing the dog paddle they cut their own throats with their sharp hooves and bleed to death. In all fairness, I have met people who claim to have seen, with their own eyes, swimming pigs. But having been raised with the notion of pigs as filthy animals that don't even bathe, I stick with the mainstream on this issue; I include pork on the grocery list, but cringe when someone speaks the word. I never say "pig" aboard a boat; "curly-tailed animal" suffices when some mention is absolutely necessary. Bananas, on the other hand, I do consider strictly verboten. Although I've never been told why, bananas are definitely bad luck on a boat. It is acceptable to say "banana" aboard a boat, but I always insist that the fruit itself be left ashore just in case I'm pushing my luck with the pork.

Sailing day, the day of the week when the boat actually leaves the dock and heads out to sea, is scrutinized by leery fishermen to insure the trip gets off on the right foot. Sailing on a Friday is absolutely forbidden. If anything goes wrong during a trip that begins on a Friday, it is considered fair punishment for disregarding the superstition. Boats and men ready to sail on Friday morning often wait until one minute past midnight, making the official departure Saturday morning. I suspect that this superstition might have been invented by some crew member not quite ready to leave the saloon one Friday evening. Regardless of its origin, most fishermen can recite a litany of mishaps for which Friday departures are responsible.

Other superstitions include never turning a hatch cover upside down. I suppose an upside-down hatch cover could be considered a premonition of an upside-down boat, which is definitely not a good thing. As for color, blue is unlucky for a boat. And, although not as bad as blue, yellow is not an acceptable hull color. Whistling aboard a boat is a real no-no, and is said to "whistle up the wind." The number 13 is always pronounced "twelve plus one" for obvious reasons.

Of the many superstitions of which I am aware, the only one that I flat-out refuse to embrace is that women are "Jonahs" (bad luck aboard boats). For seventeen years now, I have returned to port every time I have departed. This has shaken the beliefs of at least a few of the most superstitious of old sailors. One old-timer in particular comes to mind; he was enthralled with the idea of a female captain. I never learned his name, but for eight years he appeared to be logging my comings and goings, greeting me at the dock with "Hello, Jonah!" I always referred to him as "the Ancient Mariner."

At first, I considered the old man somewhat of a nuisance, constantly giving me advice on how to coil line or sharpen a knife. But, with time, I looked forward to the old man's criticisms and that look in his eyes when I returned to port that telegraphed his feeling of surprise; he often looked like he had just lost a bet. I began to enjoy his raised eyebrows. I always offered the old man fish from the top of the trip, which he never refused and I was happy to give. I liked placing fish in the gnarled hands that had for years taken, but could no longer take, what the ocean had to offer. It gave me a feeling of giving something back. Perhaps the fish given stood as concrete evidence that there does exist a woman who is no worse luck than some men aboard a boat and that some superstitions are obsolete.

A friend once suggested that I paint my own boat blue and name her *Thirteen Whistling Pigs*. I might not be as superstitious as some, but I am not crazy.

9

LOOSE
LIPS

Finding a productive piece of water and protecting it from encroachers is absolutely the toughest and most critical part of a swordfish captain's job. Competition for a berth is stiff, and not everyone is willing to play by the rules of "first come, first served" and "finders keepers." There are always those captains who ignore the swordfishing etiquette that has evolved through the years, seagoing Machiavellians who cause the rest of us to live in a constant state of paranoia, suspicious even of those whom we regard as friends.

"Friend" becomes a relative term when used among captains. We depend on one another for help in emergency situations but are also predators stalking the same prey. When a competitor asks, "Would you please move your set a few miles to the west so that I might have room to set east of you?" my gut reaction is to answer, "Go to hell. I've been

fishing here for a week, and I'm not budging."
But in the back of my mind I am aware that
I might require something of this same man
in the future. Although it is unlikely, I might
need to call on him to rescue my crew and
myself from a fire or sinking. Or, more likely,
my request might be as simple as asking to
borrow some Freon to charge my ice machine,
without which completion of the trip would
be impossible. So, if moving to the west will
not affect my productivity significantly, I will
be inclined to accommodate my "friend."

In recent years most fishermen have found
it necessary and beneficial to work together,
with open and honest sharing of information. Although there remains a peaceful com-
petitiveness among us all—everyone wants
to catch the most fish— there is none of the
deliberate sabotaging of gear or collusion
that often occurs in the inshore fisheries.
The U.S. Grand Banks fleet is as close-knit
a group of fishermen as I have ever seen.
When I wish a fellow captain "Good luck" on
the radio and tell him that I hope he loads his
boat with fish the next day, I am sincere, and
hope that only I will beat him.

"Friends" or not, we all have $40,000 and
thirty days of our and our crews' lives invested
in each trip, either of which is reason enough
to justify unscrupulous behavior. If a captain is not catching enough fish to cover
expenses, the pressure is sufficient to moti-
vate him to finagle a better spot. Because all
captains are subject to the same pressures

and know to what extremes we push ourselves, we have an inherent distrust of one another.

Even at this early stage of our trip, I was aware of who was where, what they were catching, and whom I would prefer to stay away from. I was also aware that before I worried too much about who was trying to usurp my berth, first I would have to find one worth fighting for. There was no need to be adamant about fending off the competition until I was actually located and my location proved to be valuable. The task at hand, and for me the biggest challenge of the trip, was to find a piece of water in which to make our first set.

Finding a piece of water, and swordfishing in general, has changed considerably since I first started with Alden aboard the *Walter Leeman* the summer following my freshman year of college. Technological progress manifesting itself in marine electronics is responsible for what has amounted to a revolution in the industry. The *Walter Leeman* had no GPS, no down temp bird, no Doppler, no color sounder, no video plotter, and no beeper buoys. We had no monofilament fishing line; instead, we were equipped with a twisted, three-strand, tarred type of mainline. Snaps and hooks were secured to leaders by knots; we had no need for crimps. Alden Leeman had a sixth sense when it came to finding fish, and needed only minimal electronics. He could smell fish, and often set out in a piece of water simply because it "felt right." As much time as I spent with Alden learning how to catch swordfish, the most important lesson could not be taught. Alden's fish savvy never rubbed off on me.

The most successful fishermen of my generation are pseudo-scientists, fishing gear engineers, and electronics wizards. Rather than flying by the seat of our pants, as Alden did, we study data and base decisions on statistics. We rely heavily on technology and are perfectionists about bait and tackle. I couldn't "feel" my way out of a paper bag, but with all of the *Hannah Boden*'s state-of-the-art equipment, I am always confident of exceeding even the best of what Alden accomplished in his many years of longlining. Still, if I could trade all of my electronics for some of Alden's natural ability, I would.

Alden also had a unique way of handling the occasional squabbles and problems he had with other fishermen. The distance to the nearest warden, marine patrol officer, or attorney necessitates that offshore fishermen do what Judge Wapner warns against: We take the law into our own hands. Although most of us work out our differences over the radio, I recall one instance when Alden opted for the face-to-face.

After two haulbacks slowed because we had to untangle our gear from the gear of a Canadian who had managed to set over us every night, and several futile attempts by Alden to contact the Canadian captain by radio, Alden had had enough. Midway through the third consecutive haulback, and weary from dealing with the massive snarls that occur when two strings of gear occupy the same space, Alden drew his knife. Cutting our mainline free from the boat with one quick slash, Alden vowed to "visit" the Canadian boat that now appeared only as a dot on the horizon astern of us. Although I had worked for Alden only two summers at this point, I was well aware of his fiery temper, which had earned him a nickname among the crew: "Screamin' Leeman." I had witnessed Alden's tantrums. And I didn't remember ever seeing him this angry before. Once, in a tirade, he physically ripped the toilet from the deck of the *Walter Leeman*'s head and threw it overboard because it hadn't been cleaned properly. I wondered, as we neared the Canadian boat, whether these fishermen were in for one of Alden's world-class tongue-lashings or if he intended actually to board their boat and punch them all out. Fortunately for them, neither happened.

Alden steamed the *Walter Leeman* with the throttle wide open, and eventually the tiny dot grew to a 60-foot wooden boat named *My Pal*. Alden's face was red, and the veins stood out on his neck as he eased the *Walter Leeman* alongside of *My Pal*. The Canadian boat drifted, the crew and captain lining her rail, ready to "talk." Just as we reached position

157

and were about to lay rail to rail with *My Pal*, something within the fo'c'sle of the Canadian boat exploded with an ear-splitting *BOOM* that shook both vessels. No longer lined up at the rail, the Canadian captain and crew were now as far to the stern of their vessel as they could get. Wide eyes reflected the flames that flickered through portholes and hatches. Black smoke billowed.

"Do you have a fire extinguisher?" Alden yelled.

"Yes, down there!" one of the fishermen answered, pointing to the fo'c'sle, now fully engulfed in black and orange.

My shipmate, Tim Bear, appeared at the rail of the *Walter Leeman* with a huge chemical fire extinguisher he had retrieved from our engine room. He flew over the rails of both boats, squeezed the extinguisher's handle, kicked *My Pal*'s fo'c'sle door open, and spewed the contents of the canister into the heart of the fire. Next Tim grabbed the *Walter Leeman*'s deck hose and marched down into the blaze with the 2-inch-diameter stream of salt water. Finally, Tim emerged back into daylight, totally covered with soot. Between coughs, he managed to say, "It's out." The air smelled of smoldering wood and rubber, and the only sound was that of a river of black water that gurgled into the ocean from *My Pal*'s bilge pump outlet.

My Pal was not in any immediate danger of sinking but was definitely out of commission. The Canadian captain used our radio and called a fellow Nova Scotian fisherman who was nearby. The Nova Scotian agreed to haul the rest of *My Pal*'s gear and tow her home for repairs. When the second Canadian boat appeared, we left *My Pal* and steamed back to deal with the remainder of our tangled mess. I stood on deck with the other members of our crew, and said to no one in particular, "They were lucky we were there."

Mark Leeman, a distant relative of Alden, answered with what we all believed to be the truth: "They were lucky they caught on fire. I've never seen the old man so mad."

Second-guessing one's own decisions is what captains do best, and was exactly what I was doing as the sun climbed out of the water on the horizon at my port side. Minutes turned into hours, and as the sun rose higher, so did the degree of my self-doubt about leaving the strip in search of greener pastures. I steamed south across mile after mile of flat, cold ocean, concentrating with enough intensity on the temperature gauges to push them into action through sheer strength of will. "Come up, you stupid son of a bitch," I swore at the surface temperature gauge that stubbornly refused to creep above 58.50.

I felt disgust mounting to extreme dislike of the small blue box with its red digital display, and hoped it would snap to life before it forced me to categorize it as one of my most hated machines. Because objects are apathetic about my opinions of them, threats seldom work. I had, on one desperate occasion, lowered myself to trying psychology, whispering small niceties to a generator that refused to run. The engine simply thumbed its nose at my compliments; quite humiliated, I vowed to never try that approach again.

"A watched pot never boils," I said, and forced my eyes away from the red "58.30" that lit up on the face of the gauge. I turned on the Doppler; while it warmed up, I examined the latest weather map. A weak low-pressure system with a trailing cold front was heading our way, bringing with it some rain but not enough wind to cause concern. Crumpling up the map and tossing it into a cardboard box I used for trash, I turned my attention to the Doppler's display screen.

The Doppler is the most advanced piece of electronics aboard the *Hannah Boden*. Although I have read the user's manual several times, I have never been very comfortable with the Doppler, and was not confident that I was using its full capabilities. The Doppler is used to detect and define thermoclines, layers of water, certain layers being more abundant than others in fish. The layers are quite distinct; imagine blankets of varying thickness heaped over a bed. But now imagine the blankets are in motion. Each separate layer has its own temperature and current; once the fisherman determines which layer is most productive, the Doppler is used to keep track of it. The user's manual had been translated from Japanese and left a lot to be desired. Few other boats in the fleet are equipped with Dopplers, and the captains who have them share my feelings of inadequacy.

What I do know about the Doppler is this: The Doppler works with three separate transducers, an electronic compass, and the GPS to measure the speed and direction of the current at three different depths, selected by the user. The results are displayed in numbers and compass points relative to the motion of the surface current. Relative motion is confusing. Think of the scary feeling you get when it seems your parked car is suddenly and unexpectedly rolling forward, while in actuality it is the car beside you that is moving, pulling out of its spot in reverse.

It wasn't until I took a radar course to get my Coast Guard license that I finally began to understand the principle behind the Doppler and the concept of relative motion. The motion of another vessel (vessel number 2) observed on the radar screen of your vessel is relative to the motion of your own vessel. Knowing the true motion of your own vessel and the relative motion of vessel number 2, the true motion of vessel number 2 can be determined by doing vector analysis with paper and pencil. The same calculations can be done to make sense of the Doppler's information. A fifteen-minute drift test indicates the true motion of the surface, which is the first leg of the vector. The second leg of the vector, which is supplied by the Doppler, is the relative motion of the current at some specific depth, let's say 20 feet. The final leg of the vector represents the true motion of the current at 20 feet. The speed and direction of the current at the depth where the hooks are fishing are just as important to know as the temperature of the water at the same depth. The compass roses on my Grand Banks chart are all but obliterated from vectoring, erasing, and revectoring Doppler numbers.

It is not absolutely critical that I know the true motion of the current below the surface, but vectoring has helped me better to understand and use the Doppler. Generally, readings of less than .3 knots are desirable as they indicate very little relative motion, or that the water at the specified depth is moving at about the same velocity and direction as that on the surface. Normally I would adjust the three depths at 30 feet, where the mainline lays; 72 feet, where the hooks hang; and 90 feet. When I use these three depths and get readings of velocities of less than .3 knots for each, I know that the depth of the current where I am fishing is at least 90 feet. High readings at 72 and 90 feet usually indicate slow-moving and cold water right below the surface, and this is usually confirmed by the down temp. When the tide is shallow, the thermocline thin, my hooks might hang in the cold, slower moving water while the mainline lays in water moving a full knot faster, dragging the leaders along with it, causing them to spin and twist up around the mainline, where they have no chance of catching anything.

The electronics are not always foolproof but can help me avoid some disastrous sets. The most frustrating sets are the ones that look perfect: a tight break on the surface and below, deep tide, blue water, birds and bait fish—but no swordfish on the haulback. No matter what electronics a captain has and how much know-how, you can't catch 'em if they're not there. And the only way to know whether the fish are home or not is to put the gear in the water. I guess that's why what I do is called "fishing." If it was easy, we would refer to it as "catching," and there would be a lot more people doing it. Then, perhaps, there would be reason for the conservationists and swordfish rights activists to advocate putting an end to commercial fishing. Alden once told me that he believed fishermen using only hooks and harpoons could never wipe out any species of fish that reproduce by spawning, such as swordfish. And in seventeen years of swordfishing, I have seen no evidence of depletion.

The potential fishing grounds are expansive east of the Grand Banks of Newfoundland, and the U.S. swordfish fleet relatively tiny. I can name every boat and captain in the small group. The boats are small not only in number, but also in size. Prior to 1984, the majority of swordfishing done by boats out of New England took place on Georges Bank, which lies just offshore of the Gulf of Maine. A World

Court decision to settle an ongoing dispute between Canada and the United States over fisheries management and conservation was reached in October 1984. The court's decision established a boundary line, the Hague Line, to divide Georges Bank between the two countries, the portion richest in swordfish going to Canada. As a result, many relatively small American boats are forced to travel to the Grand Banks—to fish in international water, 1,000 miles farther east and away from their home ports—in order to catch enough fish to make a living.

I have always been happy to comply with regulations set forth by our country's finest scientists and bureaucrats, and to observe boundaries, believing that laws will insure the future of swordfish and swordfishing. What annoys me are the actions taken by groups such as the head chefs of a number of fine restaurants who boycotted swordfish, taking it off their menus in their Give Swordfish a Break campaign. Give *me* a break! I wonder how these chefs keep themselves abreast of the state of the fishery and how they can be so conceited to presume they might know better than the fishermen and scientists who have been working together for years to keep the stocks healthy. In my opinion, little Chef Fancy Pants should work at perfecting his crème brûlée and leave fisheries management to those who know more about swordfish than how best to prepare it.

U.S. fishermen are not pirates. We are

among the most regulated fishermen in the world, and the penalties for noncompliance are stiff. Fishermen of my generation are conservation minded. We are also frustrated that the public is being brainwashed with misinformation by a group of do-gooders. If a problem with overfishing does develop, it is not the American fisherman who should be punished, but perhaps the fishermen from countries that currently have no regulations in place and continually exceed their allowable catch quotas. Fishing for a living is our heritage. Consumers and seafood lovers should enjoy the fruits of the labor of law-abiding and conservation-minded fishermen without being made to feel guilty. Eat U.S.–caught swordfish! It's legal!

At six-thirty A.M. the numbers on the Doppler, down temp, and surface temp all went into motion. The surface temperature rose from 58.20 to 62.50. The down temp raced up to 68.30, and the readings on the Doppler settled down to .1, .1, and .1. I continued on a southerly heading and marked our position on the chart at 46° 15' N and 42° 30' W. The surface gauge gradually climbed to 65.60, while the down temp hung around 68.30 and the Doppler held its own with steady readings of less than .3 knots. The sky was full of birds. Storm petrels and shearwaters glided low to the water, working the surface looking for something to eat. My heart picked up its pace and I exhaled a deep breath in an attempt to calm my anxious excitement. "This looks good," I whispered.

I turned the *Hannah Boden* around 180 degrees and went back across the break from hot to cold, and the numbers on the electronics responded quickly. Again I turned the boat around, and when I reached the middle of the break, where the numbers changed most rapidly, I knocked the main engine out of gear and did a fifteen-minute drift test. The results told me that the middle of the break was moving at 2.6 knots at 90 degrees, due east. Returning to the chart table, I measured the distance from my present position to where the bulk of the fleet was fishing, nearly 200 miles to the southwest. I was farther east than I would normally start a trip, and the day was young, so I decided to follow this new break back to the west until setting time, or until I found where it might make a bend, giving me a corner to fish. Finally, over 1,200 miles from Gloucester, and after six days and nights of steaming, we would fish tonight! We would fish by ourselves, on our own little sliver of the North Atlantic.

As usual, the captains of most of the boats in the fleet took turns checking in with one another on the SSB radio at ten that morning. Most reported a slight improvement in the fishing and returned back to their decks to finish hauling back. The radio fell silent for a couple of seconds, then Larry from the *Sea Lion VIII* called me.

"Hi, L.T. How's the first quarter treating you so far? Over," I answered.

"A little better than yesterday. We have our fifteen hundred pounds aboard, and still have two sections to haul. Where did you end up? Did you fish last night? Over."

"We'll be making our first set tonight. I'm on the main break, forty-two forty, on the west line. It doesn't look too sporty, but we have to get started," I said, sounding as nonchalant as possible about the piece of water I was now in so as not to pique the interest of anyone who might consider joining me.

"Okay. Well, I hope it works out for you. I should get back on deck, so I'll talk with you later. Good luck tonight. Over."

"Good luck with the last two sections. 'Bye. Whiskey Romeo Charlie five two four five." As I hung the SSB's mike in its bracket, John's voice broke the squelch of the VHF radio.

"Hey, Linda. Are you on this one? *Hannah Boden*, *Eagle Eye*."

"Good morning, John. How's it going? Over."

"Oh, it's going fine. It looks like we'll end up with around two thousand pounds for the day. Sounds like you decided not to try the strip. Over."

"That's right. I followed it out to the forty-two thirty. It gets narrow east of you, and there's not much life in it. If this break runs due west, I'll be setting just south of you and David tonight. Over."

"Yeah, we figured the main break was

nearby, but until this strip totally fizzles out, I guess we'll stay on it. The fish are real nice, just not that many of them. Over."

"All right. Well, I hope you find a few more of those nice ones before the end buoy comes aboard. This doesn't really look like much to get excited about where I am now. I'll probably be sorry I left the strip without giving it a shot, but it's too late now. I'll let you get back to work, and I'll check with you and Dave before I set tonight. Over."

"Roger, Linda. Talk with you later. Out."

Replacing the VHF's mike, I glanced around the wheelhouse at the various gauges and peeked at the radar screen. It had been a conscious effort on my part to sound less than enthusiastic about my prospects for our first set. If this berth should happen to be as good as it looked, it would be a luxury not to have to worry about the competition. Satisfied that we were still on the break, I ran below and found Kenny and Carl sitting at the galley table. Kenny was showing Carl how to do something with a piece of twine. Winding the small-diameter line around his hand, tucking the end, and winding in the opposite direction, Carl concentrated on the lesson. "Hi, guys! What's up?"

"Hi, Ma. Kenny is teaching me to tie a monkey's fist. I'm going to make some tiny ones for key chains. You want one?" Carl asked.

"Sure, I'll take one," I said, and opened the refrigerator. I pulled out a package of salami, some provolone cheese, and a jar of mustard, and laid them on the counter.

"He taught me to tie one of these, too," Carl said, holding up a small noose to show me. "You never know; we may need to do a lynching before this trip is over."

"That's not funny, Carl."

"I didn't mean for it to be."

I felt a vein pumping in my neck. I took a deep breath and chose to ignore Carl for the time being. "Kenny, get the others up and get the bait out for tonight."

"Okay." Kenny jumped up from his seat behind the table. "How much do you want thawed out?"

"The weather looks good; we'll set the whole string."

"Ten sections, right?"

"Right."

Both men disappeared as I slapped together a sandwich on top of a paper towel. I slung meat, cheese, and mustard back into the fridge and slammed the door closed. "That little shit's not going to ruin our trip," I pledged through clenched jaws. Starting tonight, Carl would no longer have the time or the energy for such baneful behavior, and would work with Peter and the rest of the crew peacefully. And I would have no time to think about anything other than catching fish. Returning to the wheelhouse, I inhaled the sandwich and continued my watch on the Doppler and gauges while zigzagging back and forth across the break. Slowly, we

169

gained ground to the west. Kenny entered the bridge behind me.

"The bait's lying in the sun and should be pretty well thawed by this afternoon. What time do you want to start?"

"Around five. Why don't you ask Ringo to have dinner ready by four-thirty, and we'll set after we eat."

"So, how does it look? Are we on 'em?"

"I'll let you know tomorrow."

"I guess we'll all know by then. What do you want to use for lights and dyes?"

"Mix up the lightsticks, mostly green and blue. For the bait, dye twenty-five percent red and twenty-five percent blue, and leave fifty percent natural."

"No green or yellow dye?"

"No. Not tonight," I said.

"Would it be okay for me to call the *Northern Venture* one night after we set out and say hello to Loren? He usually has first watch over there."

I hesitated before I answered Kenny. "Well, I guess so. If David doesn't want him on the radio, you may not get an answer. Some captains are really strict about radio silence for the crew."

"I would like to chat with him for a minute. Just curious if he has any news from home." Kenny had been a part of the *Hannah Boden*'s crew since long before I had come aboard, and sometimes I got the feeling that he thought he should have been the captain rather than me. Although experienced for his age, and quite

170

capable, Kenny was not ready to run the show. It was against my better judgment to allow a member of the crew to use the radio for chitchat, but I saw no real harm in letting Kenny check in with a fellow Newfoundlander. Loren had worked for me earlier in the season, and neither he nor Kenny had been home in several months; I thought they must both be homesick.

"Just be sure to keep the conversation short and quiet," I warned. "When I get a chance to sleep, I don't want to be wakened by you and Loren reminiscing." Some small area in the back of my mind was uncomfortable with agreeing to allow Kenny the use of the radio, but it wasn't until days later that I learned my apprehension had been for good reason. Then it was too late.

By three-thirty that afternoon we were at 46° 13' N and 43° 35' W. I completed my daily ritual of trying my unproved talent for mental telepathy using the well-worn, and seemingly one-way, lines of communication from myself to the many gods and patron saints of weather and swordfish. Due south of where the *Eagle Eye* had started setting the previous night, I pulled the boat out of gear to drift along the break and prayed that this piece of water would produce what it looked capable of. I listened as the other captains checked in on the radio. Finished hauling, all now jockeyed for position for the night's set. Fish reports were mostly in the 1,500-to-2,000-pound range, and voices were optimistic that the numbers would increase with the waxing of the moon.

If we averaged 2,000 pounds per night, I thought, we would need to fish twenty nights to receive a decent paycheck. The chance of having twenty straight nights of fishable weather this time of year was nil. To date, I had never made more than fifteen sets in any one trip, and I wondered if I would have the endurance to keep up the pace for the extra nights if needed. "Well..." I sighed. "We'll just have to get lucky and fill this old girl to the hatch cover in fifteen nights." Tuning my ears back to the radios, I listened as captains wheeled and dealed for an extra mile or two of the break. Some argued about what time to start setting, the faster boats, able to regain miles lost to the tide quicker than the slower boats, advocating an earlier start. Everything was settled relatively peacefully, the captains more accommodating than they would be with greater amounts of fish at stake.

Dinner appeared at four-thirty sharp, and by five o'clock I had eaten and checked in with the *Eagle Eye* and the *Northern Venture*, which was 12 miles north of me and getting ready to start setting on what was left of the strip, which seemed to be slowly evaporating. I stood at the remote helm station in the after part of the wheelhouse, where I could see all of the electronics, the horizon over the bow, and the back deck, where the men were all in place. Wearing full oil gear, they waited for me to give them the signal to start the set. The rain, little more than a mist, fell straight down, the individual drops too dainty to cause even the slightest interruption of the sea's mirrorlike surface. Without a ripple, the ocean absorbed the rain like a dry sponge.

Kenny stood with the first beeper buoy in the starboard corner of the stern. The beeper had been secured to the bitter end of the mainline, which had been fed from the top of the spool behind the wheelhouse and through a small hole in the forward bulkhead of the cart house. From the front of the cart house, the mainline was threaded through a steel ring welded above the stern transom. The ring's function was to keep the mainline in the center of the stern as it went overboard, so that the men did not have to chase the line from side to side as the boat made sharp turns.

Through the Lexan windows of the cart house I could see Peter and Carl facing each other across a plastic tray of squid that sat on the waist-high setting table. The mainline hung between them at chest level; each man had a box of leaders at his side. Ringo had set the two baiters up with squid, some of which had been dyed red, some blue, and some left natural, as per my instructions. An assortment of lightsticks had been placed on the table with the bait. Ringo worked in the center of the deck, bent over his vats of dyed salt water, preparing the next tray of bait. Charlie stood by the ball-drop spool in the port stern, ready with the first float.

Sticking my head out the back window, I held up an index finger, indicating to Kenny that I was not quite ready. Kenny nodded back. I intended to put the first beeper right in the middle of the break, in the hottest water I could find with the down temp. With no boats on my east or west end, I could afford to be patient. We were all anxious to get started, but I had learned from experience that the biggest mistake I could make would be to start in the wrong place. With 40 miles in which to make mistakes, I would at least have the first few hooks where I felt they belonged. The down temp read 62.00 and rose slowly as I angled out toward the warmer water. When the down temp rose to 68.60, I yelled out the back window, "Let her go!" Kenny checked the power switch on the top of the beeper's canister, making sure that it was indeed turned on, lifted the buoy up over the transom, and dropped it into the water behind the boat.

As the boat steamed away from the beeper, the spool behind the wheelhouse began to spin; the mainline was peeled from the spool and payed out in our wake. I jotted down some numbers on the first page of my fishing log and tuned in the first buoy, "1695," on the RDF. Now my job was to do exactly what I had been doing all day, follow the break to the west, crossing it at very shallow angles, from hot to cold to hot.... Until we hauled back, I would have no idea what temperature range would be most productive, so tonight I would cover all the bases. If I chose to repeat the set in the following nights, the knowledge of the first haulback should allow me to fine-tune, putting more gear where the greatest concentration of fish had been caught. I called David on the *Northern Venture* to let him know where I had started, and said that I would check with him and John at ten A.M. to exchange fish reports. We wished one another "All the best" and went back to work.

Carl and Peter worked quickly to set the leaders at the proper intervals. Carl pulled a hook from his box and baited it with a blood-red squid that was about 12 inches in length and as big around as the cardboard tube at the center of a paper towel roll. Carl laid the baited hook on the setting table as he secured the lightstick to the mono, 6 feet up from the hook. He snapped the 4-inch plastic stick, releasing the two chemicals inside and allowing them to mix, resulting in a bright, lime-green glow.

Carl gently tossed the baited hook and lightstick into the wake and allowed the rest of the leader to run through his hands and into the water. When all 7 fathoms had uncoiled out of the leader box, Carl jammed the snap onto the mainline as it rushed by him, being careful to not tow the squid through the water once the slack was out of the leader. As Carl prepared his next hook, Peter set a leader from his box. After each of the two men had set a leader, Charlie stepped behind Peter and snapped the first float, with its 5-fathom drop, onto the mainline. And so it went— two leaders, one float, two leaders, one float— for a span of fifty floats, one hundred leaders, and 4 miles of mainline. After the hundredth hook was set, Kenny tossed the next beeper into the water as Carl jammed its snap onto the mainline. When "1827" splashed into the wake, Kenny yelled up to me and waved to let me know the first section was complete. I checked the time—thirty minutes, perfect—and gave Kenny a thumbs-up sign to let him know the pace of the set was right. I filled in the second line of my fishing log and tuned in "1827" on the RDF.

Five hours, ten sections, 1,000 hooks, eleven beepers, and 40 miles of mainline later, the crew ended our first set by cutting the mainline free from the boat after the last beeper went overboard. Ringo looked up from the deck and moved his right hand in a motion that imitated a fish skipping along the surface of the water. This was his signal to let me know that he had seen bait fish around the boat as we set, and I smiled and nodded. I had seen them, too, with the searchlight and on the color sounder, a type of depth indicator, which shows on its monitor schools of fish as they pass beneath the boat. As the sun goes down and darkness falls, schools of feed and bait fish, and clouds of plankton, rise from the deep and appear on the screen like bubbles in a lava lamp. Different types of feed and schools of varying densities appear as different colors, the densest schools showing as orange or red blobs, and the less dense as light green or sky-blue. By mid-set this evening the top of the screen had been lit up with a streak of brick-red over a thin yellow line, and the bottom of the screen had been covered by a greenish blue snowy-looking mass. Abundance of bait fish in the area raised the probability that there would also be some predator, such as swordfish.

Kenny started the electric hydraulic pump with the push of a button, and Carl loosened the brake on the winch for the down temperature bird. I slowed the boat to an idle and pulled the valve to turn the winch, cranking the cable aboard slowly through the block on the end of the davit on the port stern quarter. Kenny and Peter leaned over the rail and watched for the yellow bird to near the surface. When Kenny waved to let me know that he could see the bird, I slowed the winch to a crawl, inching the bird out of the water until it hung just higher than the rail. I stopped the winch, and Kenny and Peter grabbed the bird, pulling it inboard as I backed off the valve. The men placed the bird in its bracket, where it would remain until after the gear was hauled back, and Carl tightened the winch's brake.

As the crew cleaned, secured, and set up the deck for the haulback, I turned the boat around and began to steam back to the eastern end of the gear, listening for "1695." I stayed 1 mile south of the string of gear, so as not to part it with the stabilizing birds. I steamed in the warmer surface water, hoping to pick up a little extra favorable current to the east. Running in a straight line, I am usually able to chase down the five-hour set in four hours or less. Sitting back in the chair, with my feet on the console, I looked over the first page in this trip's fishing log.

Set #1

SEPTEMBER 5			SET TIME 5:00	
BEEPER	POSITION	TEMP	DOWN	DOPPLER
1695	46° 13' N, 43° 30' W	60.1°	68.60°	.1, .1, .1
1827	46° 12' N, 43° 34' W	58.9°	59.10°	.0, .1, .4
1649	46° 13' N, 43° 39' W	62.7°	64.70°	.1, .2, .2
1920	46° 13' N, 43° 43' W	61.5°	58.80°	.1, .3, .8
1612	46° 14' N, 43° 46' W	60.3°	65.60°	.0, .1, .1
1725	46° 14' N, 43° 50' W	59.9°	68.00°	.1, .0, .1
1790	46° 15' N, 43° 53' W	59.9°	68.50°	.1, .2, .1
1690	46° 14' N, 43° 57' W	62.4°	62.20°	.1, .2, .3
1970	46° 13' N, 44° 01' W	62.2°	61.50°	.1, .3, .4
1625	46° 12' N, 44° 05' W	60.7°	67.40°	.1, .2, .1
1611	46° 11' N, 44° 10' W	60.9°	68.10°	.0, .0, .1

END SET 10:15

I was happy with our first set. The break had offered no surprises, and I didn't have any cause to experience the anxiety attacks I get when suddenly caught in some unexpected cold finger or puddle of water, wondering which way to turn to get back to the break while trying not to waste gear. I'd had no confrontations. We had run into no other boats "setting through the back door," or setting toward me in my berth, claiming not to have known

I was going to be there. Captain Asshole, when he does show up, usually appears when I have about half of my gear in the water, forcing me to end my set 20 miles short or steer 1 mile inside or outside of his gear for the remainder of my string. Whether I believe that Captain Asshole has made an honest mistake or has intentionally stolen fifty percent of my berth, I do what I can to insure that he will be well out of my way the next night. Because of good radio communication, this situation does not occur often. The few run-ins I have experienced were upsetting and not easily forgotten. Any unexpected light on the horizon or unidentified target on the radar screen is cause for panic. For now, at least, we were all alone.

One mile south of the gear, the surface temperature rose to 68.80, and I wondered what the temperature might be at a depth of 72 feet. I was pretty sure this warm surface water hadn't been there earlier. I hoped I hadn't blown our first set by not poking far enough to the south. The set I had made looked good, but so did this, 1 mile away, so close. "Too late now." I yawned. I looked out the back windows and onto the deck, where the last of the crew was hosing down his oil gear and heading into the fo'c'sle. Storm petrels were everywhere. The small black birds darted in and out of the white lights mounted in the rigging and illuminating the work area. Some perched on stay-wires, while others fluttered alongside the *Hannah Boden* hunting the surface of the ocean for scraps of squid washed from the deck and out through a "scupper," a clearing port that allows water to drain overboard from the deck. I switched on the searchlight and scanned the horizon off the starboard side. The surface was alive with bait fish, popping up, jumping, skipping, and flipping. "Jesus Christ...this looks good."

"Sounds like we're on 'em!"

"Hi, Ringo." I switched off the light and returned to the chair.

"Well, how did it look?"

"It looked good, but it looks better here, where our gear isn't."

"At least we won't have far to steam for a new spot if tomorrow doesn't pan out."

"That's looking at the bright side, isn't it?" I chuckled.

"That's me, Mr. Brightside. I'm ready to drive to the other end, if you're ready to get some sleep."

"Man, am I ready. But I think I better stay up and scope this water out while I have the chance. I probably won't have time tomorrow. You had better turn in yourself. I plan to keep you busy cleaning fish tomorrow."

"Bring 'em on. We're ready."

"Good night, Ringo."

"'Night, Ma." And Mr. Brightside was gone with one flash of a smile, down to the galley, where he would no doubt smoke one last cigarette while the others ate bowls of ice cream and unwound before climbing into their bunks. If they hurried off to sleep, the crew would get close to four full hours on their backs before I would be rapping on state-room doors and calling them to join me on deck for haulback. Tomorrow night, it would be my turn for a three- or four-hour nap while Ringo or Kenny steamed the boat back down the length of the set. The two men and I would alternate nights, having a turn every third night to stay up and drive the boat while the others slept. If it was one of my nights to sleep, whoever was to drive the boat back to the east end of the gear after the set would get a nap while the gear was going in the water, as all five men are not needed on deck while setting out.

And so it would go for nights, until we had caught enough fish to return to port. Soon the men would be blurry-eyed with exhaustion, days and nights running into and overlapping one another in one giant block of time we define as fishing. Toward the end of the fishing, I would be so deprived of sleep I would catch myself looking onto the back deck to figure out whether we were setting out or hauling back. But we had many miles of line to push and pull in and out of the water before any of us would reach the point of near surrender. Right now I could only hope for the best: two weeks of fishing followed by nearly a week of steaming.

The eyes are my body parts most susceptible to sleepiness, and as I concentrated on the temperature gauge, I forced the lids to stay open which wanted so desperately to clamp shut.

If it hadn't been raining, I would have stepped out the wheelhouse door for a face full of cool salt air to refresh me a bit, but having no interest in getting wet before I absolutely had to, and having never nodded off while in an upright position, I opted simply to stand for a while. There was comfort in knowing that twenty-four hours from now I would be briefly fast asleep; even a short nap was usually enough to recharge my batteries for another haul and set.

The beeping of "1695" grew louder and more clear with every transmission, and at two-thirty A.M. I knew I would be abreast of the buoy within the next thirty minutes. By three-thirty there would be enough daylight to start the haulback, so I would wake the crew at three-fifteen. These sixty minutes before the dawn are always the longest for me. The years of keeping this schedule had not been enough to alter my biological clock; my body desperately wanted to lie down. The hunger for sleep would grow stronger every day, and would not be totally sated for at least two weeks. The average of three or four hours of sleep a night for the crew is not nearly enough to compensate for the eighteen-to-twenty-hour days of physical labor each of them produces between sunsets, but I would not hear them complaining. Fatigue is something that is seldom discussed, or even mentioned, among experienced longliners. It was understood that each of us would be worn out and exhausted, and for the next two weeks we would talk about anything *but* sleep.

The RDF's needle swung hard to port as the series of beeps blared in my ears. I turned the *Hannah Boden* to port until the needle pointed straight up, indicating the buoy dead ahead. The crack of dawn appeared through the starboard windows as a narrow stripe of pale gray between the blacknesses of water and sky. I watched as the heavy black curtain rose steadily from the ocean's surface, the gray band widening and brightening slightly. Within minutes, all of the sky from horizon to horizon had turned a multitude of shades of gray, slate clouds against an ash backdrop. My world seemed more manageable this morning; the low clouds, close and claustrophobic, formed a dome over my private puddle of ocean. The stark white whip antenna of "1695" stood out sharply against the darker shades of sky and water, like the underside of a deer's tail flashing through the Isle Au Haut pines.

Glancing at the plotter, I saw that this end of the gear had drifted to the east 24 miles since five the previous night. We would have to hustle, and have a day free of the typical problems that can occur, in order to get the gear back aboard and steam 24 miles to the west in time to set back out by five that night. Now I fully appreciated the fact that we were alone on this part of the break. There would be no pressure to scurry back to an exact starting point; instead, I would be at liberty to start at five P.M. regardless of how much ground I might lose to the east. Tonight there would be no planning and orchestrating of a set that would accommodate a number of boats, no organizing of positions and starting times to allow all neighbors the opportunity for an equal 40-mile piece of the action. Tonight I would be free to wiggle east, west, or offshore to improve my set without worrying how my move might affect someone else. Exercising free will was a selfish indulgence seldom enjoyed in this business, and it felt good. If the fish were here to be caught, I planned to keep the news to myself as long as possible.

When the boat drew to within 200 feet of the beeper buoy, I could see the yellow flotation collar and a splash of red paint on the top of the steel canister; the rest of the buoy was hidden below the surface. Knocking the boat out of gear, I ran below to wake the crew. The presence of daylight, even in its dimmest state, worked like an intravenous jolt of adrenaline. My body recognizes dawn as the time to wake up, and I felt a surge of new energy as I skipped lightly down the stairs of the gangway. Rapping sharply on the starboard and then port stateroom doors, I called out a cheerful "Good morning, guys. Time to haul back." Voices answered immediately from behind both doors. I approached the "pit" where Carl, Kenny, and Charlie slept in the cool darkness below the boat's waterline. Calling down the stairs, I waited for some response. Within seconds a light came on, and someone called up to me that they were awake and would be ready to go in five minutes.

Passing through the galley, I turned on the coffeemaker, which had thoughtfully been set up the night before, and returned to the wheelhouse to prepare myself for what would probably be a ten-hour stint on deck. I glanced out the windows; the end beeper was still bobbing peacefully off to our starboard side in the calm gray sea.

I entered the head and brushed my teeth, one of the few rituals of personal hygiene I would observe on a daily basis while fishing. I left all of the vanity that goes along with being female on the wharf in Gloucester the morning we threw the lines. I rarely ran a brush through my hair or took the time to shower and put on clean clothes, as twenty minutes to do these would be twenty minutes less sleep I might get. Although I never much cared about my appearance offshore, I consciously avoided the small mirror that hung above my sink.

In the after part of the wheelhouse, I dug through a box of boots and oil clothes to find what would be appropriate for this warm, rainy day. Pulling on a pair of low, white rubber boots, I jerked them through the legs of my lightweight yellow oil pants. For a jacket, I chose a blue, pullover type of ocean kayaking shirt with close-fitting neoprene cuffs and collar. This suit was light and easy to work in, as opposed to the constricting traditional foul weather gear of bib overalls and hooded jacket made with a thicker and heavier rubber, which I donned only on days of extreme weather. A baseball cap would keep my hair from blowing into my eyes and face; I jammed onto my head one that I had determined to be lucky. The hat was adjusted tightly enough to prevent it from flying off and into the sea, which had stolen so many hats through the years. Last, I grabbed a new pair of gloves from the box. Fishing gear manufacturers don't make gloves small enough for women, so I use ladies' gardening gloves. The gloves I had chosen for the first haul were white, with tiny black cows printed on them; at the close of the day the palm of the right-hand glove would be worn through. By the end of the trip I would have fifteen left-hand gloves; Davy Jones's locker would have fifteen threadbare rights.

Before leaving the bridge, I turned off the RDF, marked the plotter at our present position, turned the autopilot to its "remote" setting to allow me to steer from the helm station on deck, and pushed the button to activate the deck helm's clutch and throttle controls. I then met Kenny at the bottom of the wheelhouse stairs; he was heading below to check the oil in the main engine. I stepped out onto the deck and stood at the starboard rail, waiting for the crew to join me while keeping an eye on the beeper antenna in the distance.

Peter was the first man through the fo'c'sle door. He spread his arms and burst into song exactly as he had done before every haulback of the season with the chorus of "Oh, What a Beautiful Morning" from *Oklahoma!*—but with the last line changed to reflect his beautiful feeling that we would be catching some swordfish today. His deep baritone, heavier than the moist, salt air, drifted slowly down to the level of my ears and eventually settled onto the deck, where it found its way through the scuppers and into the ocean that muffled it to silence. It was a silly little song, childish, but it had become a part of the daily ritual aboard the *Hannah Boden*, and Peter knew that I would refuse to start the haul until he sang.

"Hi, Peter! Don't let a little rain dampen your spirits!" I shouted, clapping in praise of the good luck song.

Charlie was next on deck. "Good morning, Linda. You look absolutely radiant today!" (Another part of the ritual.) "Did you get a chance to ask Bob about my raise?" he teased.

"I'll bring it up at the next board meeting," I replied.

"Thanks, beautiful!"

"Big raise Charlie, really big." The three of us laughed; then Peter and Charlie headed to the stern, where they would spend the next ten to twelve hours in the shelter of the cart house, coiling and repairing the 1,000 leaders as they came back aboard.

Kenny had gone from the engine room to the deck over my head and behind the wheelhouse. He raised the starboard bird out of the water and up tight against the end of the outrigger, where it would hang until the end of the hauling. I stood at the deck hauling station, the top of my right thigh pressing against the starboard cap rail. Reaching with my left hand, I nudged the clutch control ahead and put the engine into forward gear. I pushed the throttle ahead slightly and steered the *Hannah Boden* toward "1695" using the remote helm, a 4-inch-long stainless steel rod mounted on an electronic sending unit. The remote helm is tied in with the ship's autopilot, which changes the angle of the rudder hydraulically. Pushing the rod to port steers the boat to port, and vice versa. The helm, engine controls, and hydraulic valve for the mainline spool are all located on the forward bulkhead close together so that I can reach all three with my left hand, leaving my right hand free to "feel the line" and "grab snaps."

As we neared the beeper, Kenny, Carl, and Ringo joined me on the deck. Kenny sharpened his slime knife. Carl removed a small section of the starboard rail by pulling it up and out of the grooves that held it in place, leaving a 3-foot gap in the rail, called a door. Fish are pulled through the door and onto the deck, sparing the men the backbreaking work of hauling large fish up and over the rail to get them out of the water and aboard. Carl took his place beside me at the rail and adjusted the position of the ball-drop spool directly inboard of where he now stood. Poking me gently with an elbow to get my attention, Carl nodded toward the middle of the deck, where Ringo was stretching and bending to loosen up. "Hey, old fuck!" he called to Ringo, "that ain't gonna help. You'll be crippled by the end of the day. You're too damned old for this kind of work. Ma's gonna bury you and Kenny in fish."

Ringo stood up straight and yelled back. "I'm not too old to take care of a snot-nosed kid like you. How are you going to work all day without changing your diaper and taking your nap?"

"Fuck you, Grandpa."

I had been working with men long enough to know that this was the way many of them communicated and that nothing was meant, or taken seriously, by either Ringo or Carl. The two actually liked one another; if they didn't, they wouldn't speak at all. I slowed the boat's engine and threw her out of gear as the beeper floated leisurely down the side of the hull. When the buoy was at my feet, I put the engine in reverse and backed down until the boat was dead in the water. Carl grasped the beeper's antenna in his left hand to prevent it from whacking him in the head, and, leaning over the rail, reached the steel handle on top of the canister with his right. In one smooth motion, Carl yanked the buoy from the water, over the rail, and placed it gently on the deck between us. I grabbed the mainline, which dangled over the rail and into the water, and pulled a couple of fathoms of slack onto the deck for the men to work with. Ringo unclipped the beeper's snap from the bitter end of the mainline and fed the end of the monofilament through a block that hung over the rail at my right shoulder. Pulling the slack through the

189

block, Ringo walked aft with the bitter end to the front of the cart house, where the free end coming from the spool hung through a block secured to the roof of the cart house. Tying the two ends together with a barrel knot, Ringo cinched the knot tight, dropped the line onto the deck, and gave me a thumbs-up. As Kenny secured the beeper, turning it off and stowing it in the rack, I started to haul.

I twisted the handle of the valve control for the spool, opening it slightly. Turning slowly, the spool wound the slack mainline out of the water to a point where the line had some tension on it and entered the water at about a 30-degree angle. Twenty feet ahead of me, and 6 feet off the side of the bow, the line was pulled from the water, into the block over my shoulder, through the block on the cart house, and was spun up onto the spool, or drum, as it turned. Putting the boat in gear, and increasing both throttle and spool speed to maintain this angle and tension on the line, I steered the boat, paralleling the gear. Like a giant game of connect-the-dots, I followed the orange floats to the west.

My right hand hung on the line just ahead of the block at my shoulder, my fingers working to gauge the tension of the line as it passed through them. The first leader snap broke the surface ahead of me. It hung slack, indicating no fish. When the snap hit my right hand, I grabbed it, preventing it from traveling through the block with the line, pinched it open, and popped it free of the line. Working quickly with both hands, I wrapped the top of the leader around the "clothesline" that led from the hauling station to the stern. I clipped the snap onto the mono of the same leader, forming a loop around the clothesline, and let the motion of the boat through the water drag the leader to the stern, where Peter stood waiting for it. When the leader reached the starboard stern, Peter unclipped the snap and walked the leader around the corner of the cart house, where he handed it across the transom to Charlie. Charlie stood on the port side of the stern and swiftly coiled the leader into his box, pulling with right and then left until all 7 fathoms were out of the water. Stopping to rip the lightstick off and toss it into a bucket, and again to pull the squid from the hook and drop it into the ocean, Charlie and Peter would coil in this fashion all day, pushing themselves to keep up with the speed of the haul.

I grabbed the second snap and sent it down the clothesline to Peter. The third snap was a ball-drop, which I handed to Carl, who stood beside me at the rail. Carl turned inboard to face the ball-drop spool and clipped the drop's snap into the loop of mono that hung from the small aluminum drum. Turning the hand crank, Carl spun the drop onto the spool until the float came over the rail. When the float reached him, Carl stopped cranking, unclipped the float from the drop, hung the float on the ball storage line, and returned to my side.

I continued to haul, and soon the angle at which the line exited the water increased. I felt the tension of the line intensify as it slid through my right hand, and as the angle sharpened and the line tightened, so did my excitement. I had been through this drill thousands of times, landed thousands of fish, and each was as exciting as the first. Just a hint of weight on the mainline was enough to wind me up tight.

I slowed the engine to an idle and threw it out of gear with my left hand, still hauling the line that was now bar-tight. The line was coming out of the water at my feet, straight up into the block, when I pulled the engine into reverse and backed down with some throttle to stop the boat before we ran by what was probably a fish on the next leader. When the boat runs beyond the fish, the weight of the boat going ahead against the weight of the fish can easily tear hook from flesh, allowing the fish to swim away. And waiting to back the engine until the fish is down by the stern can result in a fish chopped up by the propeller. When fish and steel blades turning at 1,000 RPMs meet, the fish loses—and we lose. What's left of a fish after tangling with the propeller is seldom enough for a barbecue.

I slowed the spool to a crawl, easing mainline aboard until a snap broke the surface. The mainline was pulled into an "L" shape with the weight of the leader. As the boat came to a stop, I nodded to Carl, who leaned over the rail and grabbed the leader just below the snap. Standing up straight, Carl leaned into the rail with the tops of his legs and hauled the leader, hand over hand, twisting his upper body to pull with his back and shoulders. Kenny and Ringo appeared at either side of Carl, each with a 16-foot-long gaff. The gaff poles were 2-inch-diameter oak dowels, and each had a large shiny hook secured to one end. The gaffers were poised and staring into the water, looking for the fish that we all anticipated. Carl gave a long steady pull with his right hand, and the fish came into view a few feet below the surface. It was a sword. It was big. And it was alive. My pulse quickened. Swordfish are the most magnificent of all ocean creatures. A streamlined and muscular missile with a bayonet, the swordfish is strong, swift, and agile.

The fish circled, swimming under the boat as they often do. Carl held the leader, no longer pulling; he waited. When the fish swam out from under us, Carl pulled in another fathom of leader. A dorsal fin cut the surface; then hell broke loose as the fish slashed wildly with its 3-foot-long sword. The fish's bill and back were lit up in blue and purple, and its sides flashed in silver and pink. With two short jerks, Kenny and Ringo sunk their gaff hooks into the head of the fish and pulled it toward the door in the rail. The fish thrashed, and the water flew. Grabbing a 24-inch steel meat hook, I reached through the door and placed the hook into one of the fish's eye sockets. Peter came from the stern with a second meat hook, and placed it in the eye socket with mine. Ringo grabbed the bill to prevent it from slashing as we all pulled together to drag the fish onto the deck. The fish slid through the door easily, and I stood and admired it for a minute. "Nice start, about one fifty," Kenny said as he zipped the bill from the fish with a push and pull of the meat saw.

"A hundred and thirty," I said, returning to the hauling station. I used an old half of a pencil to start my tally on the white-painted bulkhead ahead of me, and wrote "130" in inch-high numbers. Unclipping the leader that had caught the fish from the mainline, I tossed the snap onto the deck and started hauling again. Kenny cleaned the fish as Ringo coiled the leader, removed the hook from the fish's lower jaw, and took it aft for Peter to deal with. A few slack leaders went down the clothesline, and another live marker was pulled through the door. The next time I backed the boat down resulted in a pair of fish on two leaders tangled together in a twisted knot of mainline, a "doubleheader" of nice pups, 80 to 90 pounds each. Both fish, barely alive, had only a shake or two of their tail fins left for fight. Carl and I each hauled a leader, while Charlie and Peter came from the stern to gaff the pups through the door and onto the deck, where Ringo and Kenny went to work on them.

Cutting the twisted leaders from the snarl with a pair of mono scissors, I handed the snaps to Peter and tossed what was left of the leaders into a garbage bin on the port side. Carl and

I worked to loosen and untangle the wad of mainline and wind it back onto the drum. If pushed for time, this snarl would have simply been cut out of the line, the two clear ends tied together, and we would be hauling again within seconds. All cut snarls would be stored, to be straightened out when the crew had time. I preferred to work the snarls out as they came aboard rather than chop up the mainline. When fishing among the fleet, and racing the clock, hauling back becomes a daily ten-hour panic scene, and snarls are quickly cut and tossed aside. Eventually, as a result of rushing and scurrying, the amount of line on the spool decreases significantly as the mountain of discarded snarls grows. The miles of line that remain on the drum become full of knots, which are undesirable because they prevent the leaders heavy with fish from sliding along the mainline as the fish swim. A snap jammed up against a knot will often result in the "pulling off," or losing, of a lightly hooked fish. As Carl and I shook, pulled, and unwound the ball of mono, the butchers each cleaned a fish and the coilers built new leaders to replace what I couldn't untangle and had cut from the snarl.

Ringo has cleaned so many swordfish through the years that he has the procedure down to a science. His technique is smooth and routine; he wastes neither time nor motion. Bill, fins, and head are severed with as many strokes of the meat saw. As these parts are cut from the fish they are thrown overboard, the second fin in the air before the first one hits the water, and the third in the air before the second one splashes. The belly of the fish is then laid open with one long smooth slice with the slime knife, from anus to between where the pectoral fins had been. Two jabs of the knife cuts gill plates from nape. All entrails are pulled from the body cavity in one bloody mass and slid across the deck and out the nearest scupper, leaving behind a smeared trail of red goo. Next, the body cavity is scraped clean of the thick, sticky mucus "slime" that clings to the inside walls; the rounded blade of the slime knife is manufactured specifically for this use. Two shallow slices the length of the backbone, along either side of it, free the "bloodline" from the inside of the fish, allowing it to be pulled out in one brown, snakelike clotted string and flung over the rail into the water, where a flock of birds will often feast on it. The carcass is thoroughly rinsed with the saltwater deck hose, completing the cleaning, or dressing.

Kenny, who is also among the best of butchers, rinsed his fish and automatically looked around the deck for the next one. Not finding an uncleaned fish, he stood and straightened his back, which had been doubled over while dressing fish. "They'll never get ahead of us this way, Ringo," he said loudly enough for us all to hear.

"Yeah. Well, what do you expect from a girl and a snot-nosed kid? We might as well go in for lunch while they finish with that snarl.

Christ, they look like a couple kittens playing with a ball of yarn. Hey, you're supposed to be *un*tangling that, Carl," Ringo teased.

"Fuck you, Grandpa." I stole Carl's line. "Why don't you two put those fish down in the hold before they start to ferment? Or maybe Snot-nose and I can do it for you while you rest; after all, you have cleaned two whole fish apiece."

"Yeah, don't strain yourself, old-timer," Carl chimed in as we shook the last of the snarl out and wound the slack onto the drum. I started to haul again as Carl helped Ringo lower the dressed-out swords to Kenny, who had climbed the ladder down into the fish hold.

Before we reached the beeper ending the first section, we landed another sword, a small marker of about 110 pounds that was quite frisky but was quickly overcome by Carl's tenacity and Kenny's sharp gaff to the back of its head. Once on deck, the fish flopped on its side, raising head and tail into the air and slapping both down, over and over, flogging the deck soundly. The flops got fewer and less vigorous, the up-and-down motion working like a pump, pushing the life from the fish, from torrent to trickle in a matter of minutes. The colors left the fish in the same way that a Polaroid picture develops, but in reverse. Sharp flashing silver lines and vivid colors yielded to fuzzy borders of blended shades of blues and purples that gave way to mottled patches of grays, blacks, and whites as the last of life dribbled from the defeated fish.

　　　　★　　　　★　　　　★

Not all fish are conquered this easily, and there are fish that will never die at the hands of man. I recalled one gigantic warrior of a sword that made the mistake of taking the bait but refused to let the mistake become fatal. Stories of "the one that got away" always include a fish of unbelievable proportion, and my story is no exception. I fought this monster with 100 feet of steel boat and the hydraulic spool for forty minutes without so much as seeing the snap of the leader that held him. I carefully hauled hundreds of fathoms of mainline straight up from the depths to which the fish had managed to dive. One by one, the floats emerged, wrinkled up like football-size fluorescent orange raisins, slowly from the deep that had sucked every bit of flotation from them. When the heavy snap finally appeared, I thought the battle was over, and it was, but the war had just begun. I fought the fish with arms, legs, back, shoulders, everything I had, never gaining more than 2 fathoms before the monster greedily took them back from me. After a few minutes of tug-of-war, I allowed one of the crew to take over for me, and another man relieved him, also becoming exhausted, and we still had not seen the fish. The three of us wrestled the fish, tag-team style, until late in the third round, when I was able to haul the leader with little effort. The fish had finally given up, I thought, and was treading water at my feet just below the surface. It was by far the largest swordfish that I had ever seen; I anxiously waited for the gaffs to be driven deeply into its massive head. My blood surged with excitement and I was intoxicated with the size of the fish now within our reach. A fraction of a second later, the fish had its head down and with one mighty swat of its tail was again the length of the leader away from me, 42 feet below the surface and well beyond my sight.

We couldn't lose this fish. This was the one that fishermen dream of, and now that I had seen it, I had to have it. Again the two men and I joined forces against the brute, and were engaged in combat for what seemed an eternity; the muscles of my arms, back, and legs were on fire. The fish couldn't go on much longer, I thought. Swords aren't known for their stamina; in my experience, man always outendures fish, especially when the numbers are three against one, and one of the men is a woman. My energy was just about gone when I finessed the fish to the surface for the second time. As before, the sword took one look at me with its grapefruit-size eye, put its head down, and started to dive. After the first fathom of mono was jerked through my aching hands, I foolishly bent the leader down over the steel rail to stop the fish from sounding. Now the relentless beast would have to swim against the entire boat. One heartbeat later, the leader popped and went slack. The fish had parted the mono just above the hook.

Disappointment weighed heavily on the crew and myself. I had underestimated the will

199

of the monstrous sword, and now rested against the rail, staring into the water where, just seconds before, lay a $2,000 fish. The five men who called me "Captain" were all that kept me from crying tears of frustration. Nobody uttered a sound. Suddenly, and unexpectedly, the giant fish shot out from under the boat and swam through the water into which we all stared. The fish swam on its side, glaring up at us with one big eye, and stayed near the surface until it was out of sight again, its victory lap completed. I felt the fish gloating in freedom and rubbing my face in defeat. The man beside me jumped up onto the rail, shot two middle fingers into the air, and hollered "Fuck you" in the direction in which the fish had disappeared. It seemed the only appropriate send-off, and we all joined him in a chorus of Fuck-yous and middle fingers. I screamed until my throat was raw.

When most people tell stories of Man vs. Nature, they are philosophical about nature triumphing, and often depict both man and beast as being somewhat chivalrous. I am afraid that I have never possessed much of that "Free Willy" spirit, and confess that I have only bitter feelings about the one that got away. Years have passed, and the recollection of losing that fish brings only two words to mind.

As I hauled the second section of gear, I thought we would surely lose a few fish this trip, mostly due to the fish being lightly hooked. When hooks pierce skin and flesh only, they are easily torn from the fish when hauled. Kenny climbed out of the fish hold, and he and Ringo slid the insulated cover over the hatch. "Hey, did I ever tell you guys about the monster sword?" I asked.

"The story with the lesson about not bending the leader over the rail to stop the fish from diving?" Kenny asked.

"Yeah."

"Only about a dozen times."

"Oh, okay. Hey, Ringo, isn't it time for breakfast?"

"I'm going in to turn the oven on right now," Ringo answered as he peeled off his gloves and headed to the fo'c'sle. Leader after slack leader went down the clothesline to the stern before I finally backed the boat down for what turned out to be a very small swordfish. The 30-pound puppy wiggled around on the surface while I decided whether to gaff it aboard or let it go free. The fish was quite lively and, being hooked around the bill, was not losing any blood. Legally, we were allowed to take 15 percent of our total head count in fish weighing less than 40 pounds. We tried to release the smallest ones and those that would survive, keeping to make up the allowable percentage only those that were dead, weak, or mortally wounded.

"Release," I said, and Carl pulled the fish through the door using the leader like a leash; he held the fish still while Kenny unwrapped the mono from around its bill. Carl gently slid the sword back into the water headfirst, and we watched as it darted away. The next leader held a blue shark, as did the leader after it and the one after that. "Oh, shit. Blue dogs." I sighed as I hauled shark number four to the surface. Carl and Kenny were both busy cutting hooks from sharks' mouths, clearing what was left of the leaders, and throwing the sharks back overboard. Ringo reappeared from the galley just as I tugged a shark over the rail and threw it onto the deck in body-slam fashion. Ringo grabbed his knife and took care of the hook while I continued to haul. Shark after shark came over the rail, a parade of demons that chewed up the gear and time. Carl yanked nearly every shark aboard. While I drove the boat, Ringo and Kenny cut the hooks from, and set free, the useless blue dogs, and Peter and Charlie struggled in the stern to keep up with repairing the badly mangled leaders they were receiving.

The back deck filled with sharks that squirmed, curled up, and rolled around. I threw the boat out of gear to give the men time to clear the deck and catch up with the leader repairs, once again thankful to be fishing alone on this part of the break. When pushed for time, sharks are cut off without being hauled aboard, and swim away with a $1 lip ring. Eventually, both hooks and mono become scarce; the lack of either can drastically impair the success of a trip. With no close neighbors, we could afford the time to save all hooks and as many leaders as possible.

While the crew worked, the boat drifted and I went topside to check the water temperature. I was not surprised to see the surface gauge at 56.80. "I guess I'll stay away from the cold side tonight," I said to myself, and looked at my notebook, which lay open to the page on which I had recorded this set. The beeper that started this section had been set in the coldest water I'd tried all night; by the end of this section, we should be out of the cold water and the sharks, as the next beeper had been launched in warmer. I returned to the deck as Kenny tossed a 4-foot shark over the rail.

"Dogged up!" Ringo exclaimed as he kicked a large shark out through the door, clearing the deck.

"Cold water. I just checked the log. By the end of this section we should be back on some fish." I turned toward the rail, put the boat in gear, and headed for the next orange float. Soon Ringo delivered our usual breakfast of hot pizza. We ate while we hauled. Carl brought a shark aboard between bites of pepperoni; by the time the last slice had disappeared, we were out of the sharks and moving quickly down an empty string of gear. The beeper ending the second section came aboard without my tallying a single fish. I penciled in a goose egg beside the "#2" on the bulkhead, and started the third section. When "1920" came aboard, ending the third section, I counted eight hash marks for the section and breathed a sigh of relief. Section four started out quite sharky, but we managed to tally two keepers, bringing our total to fifteen fish for four sections, not bad.

Sections five and six were better than I expected, with four fish each. At ten o'clock, we had twenty-three fish for nearly 2,000 pounds, and we still had four sections yet to haul. I threw the boat out of gear to drift while I ran topside to listen to the fish reports from the fleet. I asked the crew to get some bait out of the freezer for the night's set, and then to continue to haul while I checked in with John and David, and looked at the morning's weather maps.

Both radios were squawking as I entered the wheelhouse. Two captains argued on the SSB about an apparent gear entanglement that had resulted from the misunderstood, or misreported, starting position of the western boat of the two. When the problem was about to be resolved by the western boat's captain's agreeing to start 5 miles farther to the west, a third voice argued that the 5 extra miles were part of his berth and that the other two men would have to move east for more room. Of course, there was a boat to their east whose captain let it be known that moving east would not be possible, as his best fishing had been on the western end of his string, and he was indeed unwilling to budge to the east. Next ensued the ever-present argument of who had been in position the longest, who had set on this break first, and who should control the next set, longevity having seniority. I had heard, and been a part of, this discussion so many times that I knew the lines by heart.

David and John, on the strip above me, compared notes on the VHF. Both men had two sections left to haul, David with sixteen fish so far, and John with nineteen. When they finished talking, David called me and asked how we were making out. I explained that our progress had been slow because of blue sharks. With the squabbling of the SSB in the background as a reminder of how lucky I was to have the break to myself, I lied, and said I'd caught only fourteen fish so far. When pushed for details about the number of sharks, I exaggerated slightly to discourage further anyone from joining me. Next, I repeated my fraudulent fish report to someone who called on the SSB, obviously looking for a less-congested area to fish. Before I could be asked for more details and be forced to elaborate upon the lies with which I was uncomfortable, I claimed that there was a need for me to hurry back to the deck, and I signed off. As I made my way back to the deck, I thought the only thing I disliked more than lying was being stuck in the middle of several boats, unable to adjust my set in any way. For all I knew, everyone could be lying; that was my rationalization for deception.

Two small markers lay side by side in the middle of the deck, and Kenny was dragging a pup through the door as I stepped out into the rain. I pulled on my wet gloves and relieved Ringo of the hauling duties so he could clean fish. "Jesus, it didn't take you long to put three fish aboard," I said.

"We don't waste any time, Ma. What's the good word from the rest of the fleet?" Ringo asked.

"Well, John and David are doing about the same as yesterday. They should end up with a couple grand apiece. The guys to the west are doing okay too. There's a lot of pushing and shoving going on."

"We must have better than two thousand pounds now, and we still have three and a half sections in the water. If anyone knew that, they'd be on top of us."

"Yeah, you've got that right. What they don't know won't hurt us," I said, putting the boat in gear. I started winding the line onto the drum, and before I knew it we were starting the last section. I was feeling good with thirty-five swordfish and one bigeye tuna for the first 900 hooks, and hoped to snag a couple more with the final 100. The sky darkened, and the rain, which had been light all day, came down in buckets. There was no sense running for my hooded oil jacket; I had been wet all day, and continued hauling through the downpour, wanting only to pull the last beeper aboard and start the night's set.

It seemed that every time I got the *Hannah Boden* creeping ahead, I was backing her down again. Mostly heavy pups, but also a couple of medium markers, were drawn through the gap in the rail and lined up on deck, where they lay like dead soldiers waiting for burial. Carl and I smiled at one another each time another fish joined the ranks of the dead. Kenny and Ringo, hustling to catch up, never had a chance to look up from their work; each time they finished with one fish, another one slid through the door to take its place. When the final beeper came aboard, I counted fifteen hash marks on the bulkhead beside the "#10," and quickly totaled the tally for the day. "I have fifty for the day, Kenny," I yelled through the drops that pounded on all of the *Hannah Boden*'s horizontal surfaces. "Let me know what you get for a count when you pack them tonight. Carl, I'll yell out the window to you when I'm ready to launch the down temp bird. Hey, Peter, how badly did the gear suffer from the shark attack?"

"Charlie and I will have the boxes full again by setting time." Peter's voice and accent shaped his simple answer into a lyric from a calypso tune. He ducked back into the cart house to continue replacing and repairing the mangled leaders.

"Dinner at four-thirty, okay, Ringo?" I yelled to the cook, who was bent over the last swordfish on deck.

"You've got it."

Leaving the crew to take care of the fish and prepare the deck for setting out, I skipped up the stairs to the wheelhouse, flipped the autopilot on, switched the engine controls back to the bridge, and started steaming west at close to full throttle. I examined the plotter as I pulled off my wet deck clothes, hung them to dry over a railing, and kicked off my rubber boots. It was two-thirty, and we had 14 miles to go to get back to our starting numbers. Both radios were quiet, and I knew that would change as setting time neared. I flipped on the electric heater on the port bulkhead and entered my stateroom to change into some dry clothes. Peeling the wet sweat-shirt from my clammy skin and throwing it on the floor of my shower stall, I hoped that it would dry before it grew mold and started to smell.

Dry, warm, and comfortable, I slid open a back window and yelled down to Carl that I was ready to launch the down temp bird. As the men continued to work in the cold and heavy rain, small rivers streamed from the edges of their hoods and the ends of their sleeves. Although the weather map showed the end of the precipitation near, I understood that even if it stopped this minute, my crew would not be dry and warm until very late tonight, when they crawled into their bunks. The moisture from several hours of working in a cold ocean rain seeps through every pore of the skin, chilling to the deepest part of bone. Like an old wooden boat saturated with salt water, it takes a body time to dry out; it would be hours before the last shiver left the spines of the men. I also understood that the crew would work, oblivious to the weather, no matter how bad it might get, as long as the fish kept coming aboard at this pace. They were happy with our first set, and so was I.

Towing the down temp bird and watching the Doppler, I chased the break back to the west, noting that it had moved a few miles to the north. The hottest surface water was still 1 mile south of the quick break; I decided that I would not try setting any gear in it tonight but would stick with what I had done last night, avoiding only the coldest water—and, I hoped, the sharks. I considered it a positive sign that the break was moving north, or "pushing up," as opposed to "backing off," or moving to the south. Generally, when the break starts backing off, the fishing drops off drastically. As long as the break continued to push up or hold its position, I would be optimistic about future sets. I completed the first page of my fishing log with "50 Sword 1 + Big Eye = 4500 pounds."

The captains of the *Northern Venture* and the *Eagle Eye* were on the VHF and discussing starting positions. David had bombed out on his west end and wanted to shift 10 miles to the east, but John had done well on his west end and was hesitant to move. David reminded John that he had been fishing the strip two nights before John had arrived in the area and should have the privilege of choosing a starting point, within reason. The two men reached a compromise of a 5-mile shift to the east and agreed that the productive part of the strip was indeed shrinking. I marked both men's starting positions on the plotter. They, too, had moved a few miles north, leaving a healthy gap between them and us.

By five P.M. we had eaten and the crew was in position on the back deck, where they waited in the rain for the signal to throw the end buoy. We were now 7 miles north of where we had been twenty-four hours ago, and I hadn't quite made it back to the 43 degrees 30 minutes west line. With nobody fishing east of me, I was free to start short of the mark, which I did with a wave of my hand and a shout out the back window. The buoy marked "1695" plunged into our wake with a splash, and immediately the drum began spinning off the miles of mainline that we had spent all day winding up. One inch above the white line on the plotter that marked our first set, the blue blinking dot paralleled our previous path.

We had a section and a piece in the water when Kenny shouted up the stairs to me that he had completed packing the day's catch in the saltwater ice and had counted fifty-four swords and one tuna. I asked Kenny to replace Ringo on deck so that Ringo could sleep during the remainder of the set and relieve me for a few hours before daylight. Once the sky had gone completely dark, the fatigue that had trailed me all day finally caught up and overtook me like a blanket of fog, dimming my perception and slowing my movement around the wheelhouse. Ringo came up to say goodnight and delivered a much-needed cup of coffee. "Oh, thanks, man. You better turn in. I'll be shaking you in about four hours to steam back for me."

"I'm going. How's it looking tonight? Are we on 'em?"

"So far, so good. We ended up with about forty-five hundred pounds today...good start."

"Yeah, not bad for a girl. 'Night, Ma." Ringo left, and I struggled to keep my concentration focused on making a good set, and my eyes from closing. Bob Brown called on the SSB, and as soon as we signed off, I turned the volume down low enough so that I couldn't hear anyone else call me and I could avoid having to perjure myself again until the next day. Within seconds, David called on the VHF to let me know that someone was calling me on the SSB.

"Thanks, Dave. I turned it down after I spoke with the boss. The static drives me nuts when I'm trying to concentrate. I'm hoping to stay out of the damned blue dogs tonight. Over."

"We haven't had much trouble with sharks up here, but the fishing dropped off for us today. We did end up with eighteen hundred pounds, and John had a few more than that. If this water keeps shrinking, we'll be looking to relocate. How did you end up for the day? Over."

"Oh...around two thousand, I guess, but the sharks hurt us bad, chewed up a bunch of brand-new leaders. Over."

"Roger. Well, you'll probably fine-tune the set tonight and have *fifty* fish tomorrow. Over."

"Yeah, in my dreams! All right, Dave, I have to pay attention to what I'm doing here.

I'll talk with you in the morning. Good luck. 'Bye."

"Good luck, girl. 'Bye."

David's voice echoed in my head: "...we'll be looking to relocate...looking to relocate...relocate..." I realized that even an Academy Award performance disparaging the main break and inflating the number of blue sharks would be insufficient to keep the competition at bay should the strip suddenly shrink to the point of no longer being fishable. David and John were friends of mine; I would rather work with them than many others in the fleet. Although I had been on the receiving end of collusion many times, lying never set well with me. It wasn't that I didn't want David and John to do well. I did. But I've never had to remind myself of why I had spent most of the past fifteen years of my life so far away from home, at sea in a small boat. I lied for the sake of the livelihoods of my crew, my boss, and myself, but mostly I lied because I had worked long and hard to become the best, and it felt good to be number one. Getting to the top of the heap was a painful journey, and I planned to stay there. When I'd wished David good luck, I was sincere in my hope for his success, because it was his success that would ensure the status quo for at least one more night.

One night turned into four, and David and John still clung to the strip that threatened to vanish daily. They reported catching heavy markers, fish weighing from 150 to 200 pounds apiece. Big fish can be seductive, and I was confident that both men would stay with their sets until they caught the very last marker living in that precious sliver of warm water. As long as I continued to shave the numbers of our daily catch to match theirs, which I did, we could continue to enjoy the freedom of fishing alone. After four days of fishing, we had 17,000 pounds of swordfish aboard, and with the best of the moon ahead of us, we had every reason to believe that this would be our richest trip of the season. As far as the fleet knew, we were averaging 2,000 pounds a set, not enough to coax anyone to rush for the vacant berths at either end of ours.

My crew never slackened their pace. As we made set number five, I found it remarkable that with only three hours' sleep each night, they appeared to be just as fresh, their movements as quick and accurate, as they had been four nights before. The crew was happiest when they had no time to think beyond the next task to be done. Carl had no time to torment Peter or Ringo, and Charlie had no time to be sick. The men worked like well-programmed robots. I hadn't given a single order in four days. A nod, glance, or raised eyebrow was all that was needed as the men performed all duties expected of them. Dinners had been served at four-thirty sharp; when I swallowed the last bite and looked out the back window, Kenny already stood in the stern, beeper ready, waiting for the nod to start the set. Without a word from me, bait came out of the freezer every day at ten A.M., and fish came aboard steadily, the entire length of each 40-mile haulback. I was running on adrenaline, and each fish that slapped our deck pumped the level up a little higher and pushed us one step closer to our return to Gloucester.

Two sections into our fifth set, Kenny came up to the wheelhouse to say good-night and headed for his bunk. Tonight, Kenny would take a turn driving the *Hannah Boden* to the east end while I slept. I anticipated a deep and sound sleep, knowing that this was the best start I had ever had. Nearly half of what we needed for the month already lay buried in tombs of saltwater ice. The stars appeared for the first time in five nights. When the moon crept out from under a lingering cloud, it struck a beam on the sea, bright and wide, a blaze of pearly light that illuminated acres of water and sky dotted with our entourage of faithful birds. My ocean world opened up and expanded to its usual boundless size. The sun would shine on us tomorrow.

The hot surface water, which had been shy about mingling with the rest of the break, finally pushed up against it tightly, eliminating the mile of cold water that had separated the break into two parts until now. I shivered with excitement and anticipation of what tomorrow might bring in the way of swordfish. A bright, moonlit night and a few additional degrees of water temperature promised a marked improvement in our already excellent fishing. Except for an occasional and powerful twinge of guilt over deceiving my friends, everything was perfect.

In full view of my bunk, I marked time to the end of the set with each lightstick that dimmed to nothing in our wake, my body screaming for rest. I could almost feel the mattress under my back, and the melting of every tense muscle, as I anticipated the sleep that would soon take me to a brief coma. Finally, the end buoy went over the stern, the down temp bird was nested into its bracket, and Kenny stood at attention by my side, ready to take the reins. I struggled to focus the blurred face of the clock, and silently rejoiced when I discovered that I might get three and a half hours' sleep that night. Stumbling to my stateroom, I fell into my bunk, closing my eyes before my head hit the pillow. Two or three deep breaths later, I was somewhere between nodding off and that first delightful stage of sleep, when I heard Kenny calling his buddy, Loren, on the VHF. The fact that I could hear him irritated me, but I was too tired to yell to him to shut up. He would be quiet soon.

Teetering on the very narrow edge of sleep, the men's conversation faded in and out of my brain, more in tones than actual words. Loren's fuzzy voice oozed through the radio's speaker, his inflection indicating inquiry. Kenny's reply came in clear and concise syllables that hit me like a jolt of electricity. Kenny boasted, "We've had over fifty fish each set. I've packed seventeen thousand pounds so far." I shot from my bunk to the middle of the wheelhouse, where I stood glaring at my redheaded crewman. Quick to perceive my disposition, Kenny signed off with Loren and apologized for waking me.

"You idiot!" I seethed. "What possessed you to broadcast what we've been catching?"

"Oh, it was only Loren," Kenny said nervously.

Although he had certainly overstepped his bounds, I had no intention of firing Kenny. He was far too valuable, and I liked him too much. I thought, If I were a man, I would be punching him right square in the nose for his stupidity. But I felt that Kenny deserved something longer-lasting than a bloody nose or fat lip. A verbal barrage was all I could manage. My tongue was my weapon, and I brandished it.

"*Only Loren!* Loren, whose captain, and my friend, I have been lying to, and have made to believe that we have only eight thousand pounds aboard? *That* Loren? And what about the others I've lied to? Do you suppose any of them might have a VHF tuned to this channel?" Kenny was embarrassed. He had been around fishing boats long enough to know that it is a privilege of the captain, and the captain alone, to discuss with others numbers of fish caught or other details regarding the trip. He hung his head as I continued. "You are a moron! 'Only Loren'; give me a break. We'll find out tomorrow just how many others you have blessed with the truth. This area will now become the fulcrum of the entire fleet...bee-hive fishing, with the *Hannah Boden* right in the center." I paused for some response.

"I'm sorry, Linda," was all he could muster.

"Yes, you are, and if you ever get within six feet of that radio again, you'll be even sorrier." I marched toward my stateroom, stomping my feet. "If I happen to fall asleep, which is unlikely, wake me at three."

I flopped onto my back and stared at the overhead. Drowsiness had been flogged out of me with whips of anger. Closing my eyes, I rubbed my temples, which felt ready to explode. I wasn't sure what made me feel worse, the certainty that we would now have to share this productive piece of water with the competition or having been exposed as a liar. I would have to face the consequences of both in the very near future. As mad as I was at Kenny, I was just as ashamed of myself for lying in the first place. The damage had been done, and I had allowed it to happen by per-mitting Kenny use of the radio. I was so mad I was shaking, and took one more shot at Kenny before leaving him in peace until day-light. I yelled from my stateroom, "You haven't spoken one truthful word since I met you! Why did you have to start now?"

10

MUG-UP

At age fifteen I considered myself knowledgeable enough about ocean tides and currents to stay out of trouble around salt water. Although not a true scholar of hydrodynamics, I had learned the basics at an early age. I knew about the six-hour sequence of ebb and flow, and the 12-foot difference between high and low. I had felt the power of an undertow in the form of sand being sucked out from under my bare feet while I waded along the beach. I knew that low tide was necessary for digging clams and high tide best for diving from the ledges for a plunge into the icy cove.

Although I had been taught in school that the moon was ultimately responsible for the rise and fall of the tide, in my experience low tide was usually caused by some number of packages of substantial weight that needed to be hefted up over the beach from the skiff or lugged up over the ramp connecting the town dock to the float. The tide is always at its lowest point, the ramp at its steepest pitch, when the greatest number of large boxes need to go from boat to truck. It was in the summer of my fifteenth year that I first learned the complexity of ocean currents and became aware of something other than the moon that might control them.

A typical fifteen-year-old, already much smarter than either of my parents and far more capable than any of my siblings, I could usually think up a way to complete my chores more easily and quickly than anyone imagined possible. We spent summers in the light-keeper's house; there was no running water, and it was my luck to have been assigned the duty of emptying the family's outhouse. Every week to ten days, the six of us would have filled the hopper to its maximum capacity, necessitating my less-than-desirable chore, too physically demanding for the seven-year-old twins, and too disgusting for the weak stomach of my squeamish older sister. I was a natural and logical choice for the job.

The task itself was less than complicated. In fact, a strong back and some control over the impulse to throw up were all you needed to qualify for outhouse cleaner. First, you dig a hole in the woods. Having tied shut the top of the plastic bag that lines the can, you then lug the can and contents to the freshly dug hole. Next, the contents, bag and all, are dropped into the hole and buried completely with dirt. Finally, the can gets lined with a new garbage bag and replaced beneath the hole in the plywood toilet seat of the outhouse, to be christened by the first to get the urge.

Digging the hole was the hard part. Much of the island consists of two to three inches of moss over solid rock, which would resist my shovel no matter how tenacious the stroke. One fine day, after striking ledge with several attempts, I had a better idea. Perhaps the swarm of mosquitoes buzzing around my head was what inspired my brainstorm, or maybe it was the fact that I was going to be late for the nightly softball game in Kennedy's field. Forget the hole. I could simply dump the overgrown bucket of slop over the cliffs into the ocean, and no one would be the wiser. Why hadn't I thought of this before?

Dragging the sewage can to the edge of the sea was much easier than digging through rocks; by the time I reached the top of the sheerest cliff, I was convinced of my genius. Tipping the can over, I watched the green plastic mass plummet and splash. I seemed to have underestimated the strength of the bag, as it landed below me with a *plop*. Surprisingly, the bag remained intact, a perfect bull's-eye in the middle of the rings of ripples caused by the impact.

I had assumed that the height of the drop would result in enough impact to explode the bag beyond recognition; I was wrong. The plastic container of human fecal matter, i.e. bag of shit, had escaped the crash unharmed. My second hope, that the bag would sink out of sight, was also unrealized, another mis-calculation. In fact, the bag was half full of air, and it floated proudly like a big-assed bird. I threw a rock and hit the bag, changing its shape from bird to seal. The bag drifted off the shore to a distance where I couldn't reach it with a rock large enough to do any damage. Damn the tide! But I still continued to throw. A lobster boat sped by. I prayed the captain would not see the bag, not stop to investigate. My prayers were answered when the boat turned the corner into the cove and steamed out of sight. The wake from the boat bumped the bag up and down like a baby on a knee. I imagined the bag burping, emitting a putrid breath that would waft toward the open kitchen window from which I could hear my mother singing happily, oblivious to my plight.

The bag was apparently now caught in some current that carried it across the mouth of the cove and toward town. Goddamned tide! I panicked. I chased the bag toward the thoroughfare, pelting it the whole way with stones, sticks, anything I could get my hands on. My efforts to burst it met with no success. It was nearing dark now, and the bag was entering the town's main harbor on the back of an evil current. I couldn't be seen here. I couldn't take the chance of being caught. My parents would kill me. I turned my back on the bag and walked slowly toward home with an image in my mind of a friendly sailboater innocently gaffing the bag to do his part to keep America beautiful. What a surprise he would have.

I didn't sleep well that night. I imagined knocks on the door from angry townspeople and visits from scientists who had run tests, tying the contents of the bag unquestionably to the Greenlaws. I wondered if the bag might return to our shore, like a homing pigeon, and how I might explain its appearance to my folks. I spent several days after the incident consumed with worry. I studied clumps of seaweed and pieces of driftwood as they rode the tide in and out, back and forth. And although I was confident that I now had the tide figured out, the next time I emptied the outhouse I dug a hole.

11

THE GOLDEN HORSESHOE

Pervasive among longliners is a peculiar mindset I call "the fishing mentality." The crux of the fishing mentality is to be suspicious of good fortune, be it in the form of prolonged sunshine or copious pounds of fish, never accepting it at face value. A stretch of unseasonably fair weather is often greeted with skepticism, perhaps verbalized in a manner such as "We'll pay for this later."

The powers that be are known by fishermen to be somewhat whimsical in their doling out of good and bad, which accounts for our general distrust of any situation that seems remotely copacetic. Captain and crew often tiptoe around as if walking a thin line, afraid of doing anything that might upset some precarious balance and tip the scales from stability to doom. The majority of fishermen have learned the hard way not to boast, gloat, or even mention a pleasing situation for fear of jinxing themselves, summoning a flood tide of misfortune. My old friend Alden took this one step further; he would neither shower nor shave during the course of favorable fishing and weather, and also forbade the crew to do either. In his mind, he was doing everything in his power to maintain the status quo. From a distance, this reeks of lunacy, but when you are in the company of those whose lives and livelihoods can be, and are, determined by quirks and twists of fate, you embrace the mentality like a religious faith. I once wore the same purple T-shirt for twenty-two consecutive days, even sleeping in it, because it had proven itself to be lucky. At the end of that trip I mistakenly laundered the shirt, stiff with salt, rendering it limp and threadbare. Both salt and prosperity gurgled down the drain with the soap bubbles.

Naturally, the opposite is true. When pummeled with the slings and arrows of outrageous fortune, a fisherman will try anything to bring about a reversal. Some attempts to change one's luck might be regarded as outlandish or even cruel, but those of us familiar with the fickleness of fate understand that there exists no action too bizarre. Years ago, in the midst of a shark-infested sea, with hooks and mono dwindling into near extinction, I witnessed an exorcism. Actually, it was more of a blue-shark sacrifice; the intention of my overzealous crew was to chase, scare, voodoo, whammy, or hocus-pocus the population of menacing predators away from what remained of our beloved gear. A 7-foot blue shark was hung by a noose from the *Hannah Boden*'s rigging, where it thrashed wildly. Swaddled in rags saturated in lighter fluid, the shark was slashed at with knives and poked with gaffs like a giant piñata until a single match set it ablaze. Slowly, the thrashing reduced to a writhing, and finally a slight squirm. The fumes of blackened flesh, a strangely satisfying stench, brought hope to the men discouraged by the lack of swords and the abundance of teeth. The crew's hopes died with the flames, as more sharks were wrestled from the water and onto the deck, but hope was rekindled when the next 7-footer was drawn and quartered to try to charm the fates.

In the case of our present trip, things were happening so fast that I hadn't had time to put the fishing mentality into play. Not just fishing and weather, but every aspect of the trip had been extraordinarily good. But somewhere, suppressed in the farthest reaches of my mind, lay the mentality.

Kenny moped around the deck like a scolded puppy the morning following his radio indiscretion. My temper still frothing, I slashed at Kenny every chance I got with razor-sharp comments. He displayed a constant wincing expression and downturned mouth. So much of my morning was devoted to making sure that Kenny was miserable that I was stunned to learn that we had landed forty-six swordfish by nine A.M., with just half of the gear hauled. However, the morning's success did little to soothe the smoldering in the pit of my stomach, and, in fact, seemed to fan the fire that burned hotter and deeper with each passing minute. Each second served as a reminder of what little time remained until the morning radio check with the rest of the fleet.

My anxiety about the possible and well-deserved confrontations that probably lay ahead, now that my fellow captains almost certainly knew I had misled them, peaked exactly at ten when I threw the boat out of gear and shouted, "Hey, Kenny! It's time for you to get on the radio and announce to the fleet that we're having our best day ever. They had better hurry to this spot before we catch 'em all." Wringing the water out of my red-and-white flowered gloves and throwing them onto the deck, I leered at Kenny one last time before turning toward the fo'c'sle door and the now-dreaded radio.

"How did Kenny manage to make it to the top of your shit list, Ma?" Carl asked as I brushed by him at the rail.

Except for Kenny, all stopped working, and ears perked up to hear what had been the cause for my berating of their shipmate and friend. I paused for a second, allowing Kenny the opportunity to answer Carl's question himself. When Kenny refused to look up from his work, I decided that I might find one last thread of satisfaction in humiliating him prior to my own impending humiliation. "He sent everyone within radio range engraved invitations, welcoming them to join us in this piece of water and share in the festivities," I snarled.

"Well," Ringo said as he straightened his back, which had been doubled over since daylight, "it looks like a party to me." He nodded toward the northwest, and all eyes followed his to the two boats steaming toward us in the distance. The first vessels we had seen in nearly a week were not welcome sights. I could tell from their size and shape, and because they always traveled together, that the two boats were the sister ships from Ocean City, Maryland, *Maryanne P.* and *Leslie Lisa.* Their captains, George and Tommy, represented the ruffian element in our otherwise quite respectable group of swordfishermen. The boats had obviously never been properly maintained; they were rusty and their rigging was crude. It had been said of the pair that the ends of their trips were never determined by the filling of their fish holds but rather by the depletion of their Budweiser supply. The status of the ships' stores was often the topic of conversation between the two, beer being referred to as "canned goods."

"Oh, Jesus...there goes the neighborhood." My concern suddenly switched from my loss of credibility and the number of boats that might join us to the quality of the company we would be keeping in the days to come. Calamity seemed to pursue these two men, and, in my opinion, was often satisfied.

"We don't need to worry about those two clowns," Ringo interjected. "Neither of them could catch a turd in a septic tank."

"No, they'll just be in our way, more of a nuisance than anything else." Frustration with the events of the last twelve hours overwhelmed any excitement I might otherwise have felt for what was shaping up to be the best day of fishing I had ever had. If there had only been some way of knowing that this day was a high point of my fishing career, perhaps I would have known enough to enjoy it. I would have praised Mother Nature for the fine stretch of weather that would soon end. I would have thanked the fish gods for their generosity, the abundance of which I would probably never receive again. And I would have appreciated and nurtured the crew's enthusiasm and good spirits.

Imagining the many ways in which the approaching captains, George and Tommy, could hinder our ability to catch fish just by being themselves and being in the area, I threw back my head, closed my eyes, and laughed in total resignation. When I opened

227

my eyes, Ringo had stepped into my spot at the rail to resume hauling the gear, as he had done every morning at this time. The other men were busy coiling, pulling, gaffing, and cleaning as I trudged up the wheelhouse stairs to exchange phony pleasantries and adamantly try to protect my 40-mile claim from two of the biggest screw-ups east of Cape Hatteras.

The radios were uncharacteristically quiet, except for the ever-present static of the SSB, which would irritate anybody unaccustomed to the noise. Deciding to deal first with the vessels now bearing down on us, I called the *Maryanne P.* on the VHF and was surprised when George answered in his sleepy voice after only one call. Captain George explained, between yawns, that both he and Tommy were making the first sets of their trips this evening and that their intention was to fish either end of my gear. George would be to my west and Tommy to my east, making what he jokingly called a "Linda sandwich." When he inquired about the day's haul, I answered truthfully, reporting sixty-two swordfish landed, with over three sections yet to haul. George's next transmission was a mishmash of exclamations of excitement, prolonged silences, one long reedy inhale, a loud and raspy exhale, and a couple of dry coughs. When I continued, I gave George a tentative starting position for my night's set and explained to him that he would have to steam west, in the direction from which he had just come, 35 miles beyond my starting point, before setting west himself, in order to leave room for my gear. A moment of silence was followed by a series of short, wheezy hacks and wet-sounding snorts, and a "Well, shit, I better get going!" And off he went, leaving a cloud of black smoke above his well-rusted stern.

A similar conversation with Tommy confirmed that he would indeed fish east of me, starting where I planned to start and setting in the opposite direction. Hanging up the mike, I watched the ragged boats slink away looking like an ugly set of bookends.

No sooner had I released the mike, when I received my first jab over the SSB. It was L.T. on the *Sea Lion VIII*, his voice, loud and clear, obliterating all static. "*Hannah Boden*. Come in, Captain Sandbagger."

I felt my cheeks flush as I hesitantly reached for the mike. I could have pretended to not hear him, but knew that I must eventually answer to my friends for my deceit. Shrugging my shoulders, I answered the call. "Captain Sandbagger back. What's happening, L.T.? Over."

"Oh, not much. We're over here catching our measly two thousand pounds for the day. You know, you must have a problem with your radio. It seems to divide the number of fish you catch in half. Over."

"Yeah, I know. Don't worry, my engineer took the fish filter out of the transmitter, so it's fine now. We sure got lucky with the set last night..." I quickly changed the subject, and hoped that L.T. was ready to let it go too.

"Sixty-two fish so far this morning. We've got company for tonight though, George and Tommy. I hope the fish keep biting. Over."

"Yeah, if anyone deserves it, you do. Over."

I wasn't quite sure whether the "it" that L.T. felt I deserved was the great fishing we were enjoying and certainly deserved for the immense effort we'd put in, or my new companions, my reward for lying. Nonetheless, I thanked him anyway, wished him luck, and signed off quickly. Before leaving the wheelhouse for the deck, I listened with interest to the next conversation; I was the topic. The two distant voices sung my praises, acknowledging the successes I had achieved over the previous few years. When I'd first become captain of the *Hannah Boden*, my initial success had been met with "not bad for a girl" type comments. But now, it seemed, I had become "the captain to beat," and not many were coming close to my marks.

I reveled in their accolades, virtually wallowing in compliments until I thought my head would burst. The praise continued, with more captains joining in. Glued to the radio I had been so keen to avoid, I couldn't bear to tear myself away from the angelic voices to return to my job on deck. The words were like medicine, healing my sore hands and fatigued body. I was fresh and new, ready to take on the world, or at least George and Tommy. One final bravo and I would return to the deck. "...Yeah, she's got the golden horseshoe, that's for sure..." There it was, cold and hard:

the golden horseshoe theory of fishing, a dose of reality forced down my throat.

The captain landing the greatest amount of fish at any given time is said to "have the golden horseshoe." Unaware of when, or with whom, the phrase originated, I had been hearing it since I started fishing. Through the years, and due to the crude nature of fishermen, the phrase had been modified slightly. The top-producing skipper was now said to have the golden horseshoe up his ass. Since gaining possession of the horseshoe myself, I had preferred to think of it as being under my pillow, but no matter; the theory is based on the principle of "what goes up must come down." It was the coming down part that quickly deflated my head and spirits. The mention of the horseshoe reminded me that before receiving it I had long been without it, and that it could suddenly and without notice transfer to someone else. Without the horseshoe, I would be in the mediocre-catch category with L.T. and the others, scraping together a "measly" ton of fish a day. The thought caused me to shudder. The fishing mentality hit.

Yawning, I rubbed my eyes with the backs of my throbbing hands and returned to the deck. I wiggled my stinging fingers into wet gloves, tapped Ringo on the shoulder, and stepped in to replace him at the rail. I could scarcely creep the *Hannah Boden* ahead before backing her down on the next fish. I waited anxiously for the abrupt ending to the flurry of fish. I looked yearningly to the west for the black clouds and windswept sea that should soon dominate the area. My anger now evaporated, Kenny was no longer a target. What was left of my boggled mind was now occupied with the expectation of an onslaught of rotten luck. I listened with certainty for the light tinkling music from my childhood's Saturday mornings that foreshadowed the entrance of the cartoon fairy. Soon the fairy would flutter in front of me and write "the end" across the sky with her magic wand, concluding this episode. I waited. But the music would not be heard today. The sun continued to shine, and there seemed no end to the fish.

With less than half of a section of gear remaining to haul, I penciled in the hundredth slash mark on the day's fish tally. The jab of the pencil that made the period on my exclamation point punctuated my feelings of impending doom. In keeping with the fishing mentality, the better the good times, the more severe the bad in return. The men guzzled celebratory Coca-Colas to commemorate the landmark triple-digit addition to our fish hold. Charlie offered me a can of diet Pepsi; I was less than polite in my refusal. I cut the ovation short, mentioning the fact that they were surely jinxing the night's set by tempting the fates that patiently waited to jerk the rug out from under us. "Come on. Let's whip the rest of this gear out of the water. Back to work! We need to get steaming. I have to man the radio to keep those two morons from friggin' up our trip."

"Why so glum, Linda?" Charlie asked. His blue eyes had regained some of their twinkle, and his beard had grown to a length beyond scruffy. "We've got nearly twenty-eight thousand pounds aboard! We'll be going home soon if the fish keep biting."

"That's a big if. Remember the halibut disaster?"

"How could I forget it? What a nightmare..." Charlie scowled and returned to the cart house to coil the last of the leaders as we hauled the final 2 miles of gear.

It is often said of fishermen, and others who are drawn to a life on the water, that we have been "bitten by the bug," or that we suffer from a disorder called "sea fever." In the instance of the halibut disaster, the bug that bit me must have been a tsetse fly or some other disease-carrying insect. We left the frosty dock in Gloucester late in February with great hope and fresh enthusiasm for a fishery that we had yet to exploit. Stories from the past, of Bob Brown's loading the *Hannah Boden* to her capacity with the giant and high-priced flatfish, danced like the legendary visions of sugarplums. I was as excited as the crew to try something different, and had absolutely no idea of the odyssey that lay ahead.

The five-day steam to the western portion of the Grand Banks was uneventful. The first few halibut sets, which are a relatively short 6 miles and can be completed two or three times a day, were like a dry, nagging cough, a symptom of a more serious underlying illness. The malady persisted for two weeks, the fishing poorer than I could ever have imagined. The west side and southern tip of the bank were diagnosed as chronic. The third week of the trip, which we originally thought would be spent steaming home with the mother lode, was instead spent probing the east side of the bank and circumnavigating the Flemish Cap, both areas proving themselves terminal. For days we set, hauled, and moved; set, hauled, and moved. Each move to a new area offered hope for a cure, but our hopes went unrealized.

The trip lingered into the thirty-day mark, the empty hooks festering sores. The total depletion of the Marlboro supply inflicted new pain in the crew, all of whom were heavy smokers. Food took the place of cigarettes, and by day thirty-three the ship's stores had been reduced to coffee, canned beets, and bags of dry beans. Beets and beans were plentiful because both are purchased every trip and are seldom eaten. It became apparent that nobody aboard liked canned beets or bagged beans. Dark moods ensued as the crew struggled with nicotine withdrawal and gnawing hunger. A fistfight broke out when it was discovered that someone had devoured a can of chocolate frosting that was being saved as a coffee sweetener; the maple syrup was long since gone, following the exhaustion of both brown and white sugar supplies.

One man emerged from the engine room on around day thirty-eight with a cigarette he had found in the bilge. Cradling the cigarette like a Fabergé egg, he cried, "I don't know whether to smoke it or eat it!" Someone produced a lighter, and all hands enjoyed a couple of drags, which seemed to help morale temporarily.

We had covered 500 miles of bottom, each of which had been barren. We were fishing in a desert. On day thirty-nine, I went into a self-imposed quarantine after overhearing one of the crew refer to me in less-than-endearing tones as "Moby Dickless." I was all that stood between the crew and their homecoming, and as strong as their desire was to return to Gloucester, mine was stronger to catch enough fish to cover the trip's expenses, thus avoiding a "broker," any trip in which the expenses are not met and no paychecks are earned. I wanted desperately to forgo the shame associated with returning to port penniless, and clung to the hope that fish were around the next corner, although we were nearly out of corners to turn.

I remained in the sanctity of the wheelhouse until I successfully bummed a carton of foreign cigarettes from the captain of a German factory trawler working in the same area. The cigarettes, when smoked, smelled like burning cow manure, but their acquisition bought me some time. The crew was momentarily placated. I would make one last attempt to breathe life into the trip. From my personal locker, I dug out a small red book: *The North Atlantic and Gulf of St. Lawrence Fishing Grounds*. The boss had loaned it to me for the trip. The book, which I had considered an artifact belonging in a museum, contained fishing statistics from as far back as 1870, and nothing more recent than 1935. I flipped through the pages, searching for the copy of a map of the North Atlantic Ocean on which Bob had pointed out to me a piece of fishing bottom not included on contemporary charts. Ethel Laurel Bank, drawn well east of anywhere we had been this trip, was my last desperate hope. When Bob had first brought the map to my attention, I thought sarcastically, Oh, sure, Ethel Laurel Bank exists. It has somehow gone unnoticed for the last century, over-looked by modern chart manufacturers. Now, perhaps delirious with sea fever, I thought Ethel Laurel looked pretty good. With the carton of cigarettes as a bargaining chip, I was able to get the crew to go along with a search for the bank; in return, I conceded a forty-eight-hour time limit. If the mysterious piece of ocean bottom was not found in the next two days, I would give up and head west.

As the last few grains of sand were funneling into the bottom of the two-day hour-glass, I was busy figuring out a way to squeeze the crew for an additional day's search for Ethel Laurel. While I ran different scenarios in my mind, Bob Brown's voice beckoned me to the radio. Bob had been suggesting every night for the past five that I call it quits and come home and regroup. This evening his suggestion was not a suggestion but a direct order to return his boat to Gloucester immediately. There was some mention of beating a dead horse. The crew was relieved to hear that Dr. Kevorkian had finally stepped in and put an end to their suffering. The odyssey was forty-seven days from dock to dock; two of the men actually kissed the ground on which they first stepped after disembarking from the boat. Most of my crew quit after that dread trip, vowing never to step foot aboard a boat again, cured of sea fever, the one ailment I have never quite shaken.

The last beeper buoy landed on the *Hannah Boden*'s deck with a clunk and brought back the optimism that I had somehow lost; confidence quickly displaced discontent. Shouting a few words of instruction to the crew, I bounded up the stairs to the wheelhouse, where I peeled off my oil clothes and headed the boat in the direction of our probable starting position. Unsure of the exact number of fish we had caught, I reported to several interested captains an honest tally of a little over one hundred. As I spoke the words, the excitement mounted within me. Maybe the crew was right, a few more days like today and we would be on our way home with not only our best trip of the season, but also the shortest.

David, on the *Northern Venture*, congratulated me on the day's catch and said that he was now heading for the dock. Having a good trip aboard, he wanted to land his fish in Gloucester before other big trips started coming ashore in the days following the last quarter of the moon. It was a prudent move, I thought, as the heavy hitters hadn't been very talkative on the radio recently. Some of the top-producing boats of the fleet were on a schedule similar to mine. Soon I would have to think about when to head in myself, to avoid landing on the same day as the *Seahawk*, *Allison*, *Eyelander*, and *Miss Millie*, any of which were capable of flooding the market and deflating the price.

My immediate goal was to ride herd on my new fishing buddies, George and Tommy, keeping them at a safe distance from my spot. I called to check on George's progress back to the west, but got no answer. After several tries, I gave up on George and called Tommy. Getting no response from him, either, I sat back and watched the two targets 12 miles west of me. Like Siamese twins, the pair meandered to the west on my radar screen. I couldn't help but wonder what George had been thinking when he steamed 30 miles beyond where he needed to be, only to turn around and chug back against 3 knots of tide. A rough calculation in my head told me that George would not be in position to set out until nearly ten P.M. After setting and steaming back to his east end, he would not be able to begin hauling until six A.M. at the very earliest.

As I heard John's voice break through on the

VHF, it was apparent that I was not the only one considering George's schedule. "Sounds like George will have a long night. Over."

"Hi, John. I was just thinking the same thing. How did you make out today? Over," I asked.

"Not too sporty. I was going to jump in east of you to finish the trip, but I heard Tommy saying that he will be there. I guess you'll have plenty of help tonight, so I'll give this strip another shot. Over." I could hear a hint of frustration in John's voice. He had waited one night too long to make a move.

"Well, George and Tommy aren't known for their longevity. You may not have to wait long for a spot down here. Over."

John, who is as well acquainted with the pair as I am, probably knew that the chances were slim of either of them making the same set twice. My remark about the duo's lack of persistence was an understatement; in fact, John would not have to wait long at all for both boats to be out of the picture. The "Linda sandwich" the three of us made would soon be destroyed, as both slices of bread would peel away, leaving the meat alone. Within twenty-four hours, the captain of the *Eagle Eye* would have all the room he needed.

The evening's set went smoother than I had expected. Tommy and I lined up on the break and set in opposite directions, as planned. George steamed ahead of me. Two sections

239

into my set, the down temp indicated a layer of ice-cold water at the depth where my hooks dangled. Although the surface temperature looked good, 62 to 68 degrees, the climate at 70 feet below the surface was a chilly 54. I quickly turned the *Hannah Boden* hard to port, hoping a southerly track would produce a warmer thermocline. Twenty minutes passed and the down temp never budged, every second that ticked another possible blue shark. Perhaps I was in the middle of a cold finger of water pushing down from the north into the warm water; if so, the quickest relief would be to cut directly across it, a westerly heading. Or maybe I was already near the southern end of the cold piece and should continue running south for the warm. Compromising, I headed southwest and waited. Another twenty minutes passed before the gauge climbed out of the refrigerator, and I was now confident that the hooks going over the stern would come to rest in a spot where swordfish might feed. Ten miles south of the previous night's hundred-fish track, the odds doubled against a repeat performance in the morning. This water, which I had become so familiar with over the past week, had changed drastically in the previous twenty-four hours. I was afraid that the change could not possibly be for the better.

Making the best I could of what the ocean had to offer, I zigged and zagged my way to the west, steering clear of the cold water for the rest of the set. I called Tommy to see if he had encountered the same problem. He replied that his down temp bird broke three years ago; because he considered it a pain in the ass to launch and retrieve it every day, he never bothered to have it fixed. Tommy had no idea what the temperature of the water was below the surface, and couldn't have cared less. Being as diplomatic as I could, I suggested to Tommy that he set some gear in the flat, hot surface water to minimize the probability of a shark attack his very first set. I warned him that we had found the sharks both plentiful and voracious. I could tell from his reception of my suggestions that Tommy didn't trust me and had no intention of setting south of the surface break, which did indeed look inviting. Tommy politely told me to mind my own business, which I did.

"Hey, Ma! Is he paranoid or what?" Ringo laughed from the gangway. He had obviously been there long enough to overhear my conversation with Tommy.

"You know, I lied about what we were catching the first few sets, but I would never intentionally sabotage someone's trip by directing them away from the fish. We'll be hearing ol' Tommy cry tomorrow when he's being devoured by the blue dogs."

"I doubt we'll hear him cry. He'll just pop a can of Bud and take a nap while his crew fights the sharks!" Ringo sighed before continuing. "Well, that's their problem. Our problem is that we didn't thaw out quite enough bait for ten full sections. It looks like we'll just make it to nine and a half. Okay if we cut it off a little short tonight?"

I knew that the rest of the crew would be hoping Ringo would return to the deck with permission to end the set a few minutes early. I also realized that Ringo knew full well what my answer would be before he asked. My reply took no thought or consideration. It was by rote. "We will set the full string every night that the weather allows us to do so. We're here to catch fish. It won't take long to thaw out a box of squid in seventy-degree water."

Ringo smiled and shrugged his shoulders in a "hey, it didn't hurt to ask" manner, and disappeared. I heard the bait freezer door slam closed, and watched as Ringo placed one 40-pound box of squid in a plastic tray in the middle of the deck below me. As he ran the deck hose onto the frozen block, Charlie poked his head around the corner of the cart house to see what word Ringo had received. The box of squid was Charlie's answer, and I was able to read his lips as he said "Oh, shit" and ducked back behind the bulkhead.

The salt water hit the frosty block of bait and ricocheted into an umbrella shape onto the deck. The outside sheet of ice melted, exposing the backs of the squid. Their skin, translucent, revealed wide strips of the blackish purple ink contained within each tubular body. Ringo worked with gloved hands, separating into distinct and uniform single baits what had emerged from the freezer a solid, glacial rectangle.

One by one the squid plunged into the wake behind the *Hannah Boden* until the final section had been completed. It was now time to steam back to our gear's eastern end; I did so in the absence of the light of a moon that was three nights into its waning phase. When we picked up the end beeper to begin the day's haul, the weather started on the gradual but steady decline that had been promised by the most recent surface analysis and confirmed by the barometer. The weather map showed a rather large and slow-moving low-pressure system wandering our way, intensifying as it grew closer. Although daybreak was far from sensational due to dark clouds that masked the sun's rise, if the weather map was right, the *Hannah Boden* had a front-row seat for a show that would begin this evening. The program, fresh off the fax machine, promised to be one of Mother Nature's more accomplished performances.

There was nothing remarkable about the weather conditions or the fishing for the first three sections of gear hauled. Both were satisfactory; by seven A.M. it was clear that we would have neither another hundred-fish day nor a disastrous one. Things in general were just okay—until the *Maryanne P.* steamed into sight, heading toward us from the west. I found it strange that George was at least 20 miles east of where his gear should be, and immediately imagined the worst. Perhaps Tommy was in some kind of trouble and in need of assistance. As we continued to haul our gear,

George and his rust bucket rambled on by, trailing the familiar stream of black exhaust. Curiosity finally got the best of me. I asked Ringo to take over at the controls while I radioed Captain George.

My curiosity moved further toward concern when I was unable to raise anyone aboard the *Maryanne P*. I tried several channels and frequencies on both radios, but there was no answer. Having a boat steaming by at such close range and not being able to contact anyone onboard is always cause for worry. This situation, which seldom occurs, raises the question "Who's driving the boat?" I gave George the benefit of the doubt and assumed that whoever was on watch was either checking the engine or down in the galley making a quick sandwich. I radioed Captain Tommy, who answered promptly.

"Hey, Tommy. What's shakin' to the east? Over," I asked, relieved that he had answered.

"Not much. Fuckin' sharks." A loud exhale and cough were followed by human tones that actually resembled the English language. "I just came up to the wheelhouse to relax for a minute. What's happening with you? Over."

"Well, George just went by us heading your way, so I thought I would check and see what was up. He's a long way from where he set last night. Have you spoken with him this morning? Over."

"Nope. He won't be on the radio until ten. Over."

"Roger. I'll check with you both at ten. I hope

244

you get out of the sharks soon. 'Bye." I bit my tongue before it could add "I told you so!" and returned to the deck, where I resumed hauling the gear. Except for the unsolved mystery of what George was doing, the morning was routine. The gear came aboard effortlessly. Breakfast pizzas appeared and disappeared. I noticed that Peter and Carl were successfully avoiding one another; other than an occasional sneer or snide remark, there was no evidence of a problem. We were catching a fair number of fish and an occasional shark. Then George again appeared on the horizon. The *Maryanne P.*, this time at our stern and heading west, soon closed the gap between us, passed within 100 yards off our starboard side, and faded out of visibility to our west.

My feet hit the top of the wheelhouse stairs just as the clock read "10:00"; George and Tommy were in mid-conversation on the VHF. By the end of George's first full transmission, the situation was clear. It seemed that at some time during the *Maryanne P.*'s steam to the east end of her gear, both the wake-er and the wake-ee for an early-morning watch were asleep, the wake-er obviously turning in before the wake-ee actually took over. With crew and captain sound asleep, the boat traveled east, beyond the end of the gear and beyond us, until nine A.M., when George woke up to discover that no one had been driving the boat. George's displeasure with his crew was demonstrated by both his tone and his referring to his men as "these fucking jerks." At this rate, George wouldn't begin to haul his 40 miles of gear until noon, probably ruining any chance of setting back out tonight. On and on, the two captains lamented their poor starts: Tommy distressed about the shark population and George about his lackadaisical crew. I found myself sympathizing with them and feeling quite bad about their plights. George's final transmission negated any compassion I was feeling. "It's a good thing I drank a six-pack while we set out. If I hadn't gotten up to take a piss, we could have ended up in fuckin' Ireland."

I returned to the deck to recount the sagas of George and Tommy to my men, who were curious as to why they had seen the *Maryanne P.* pacing the ocean this morning. The crew, who found more humor in the situation than I did, bestowed upon George a nickname; from that moment on, we all referred to him as "Rip Van Tinkle."

After completing our haul, I was not surprised to learn that Tommy was already steaming west to relocate, taking a night off from fishing. The blue dogs had decimated Tommy's gear. His crew would be busy rebuilding 700 leaders while Tommy put as many miles as possible between the *Leslie Lisa* and the pool of circling sharks to my east. The *Eagle Eye* was quick to fill the spot vacated by Tommy. Armed with a working down temp, John was confident that he could sidestep the sharks for the few remaining sets of his trip.

The number seven, regarded by many as

lucky, was not for those of us aboard the *Hannah Boden* as we made our seventh set. Forced to work around George, who was only midway through his haulback and had drifted with his gear well into my berth, we experienced a turning point with set number seven. Perhaps we had gotten too close to the *Maryanne P.*, and some of her bad mojo had found its way onto the *Hannah Boden*. As soon as we set number seven, the weather went sour, stayed that way for days, and our daily fish tally dropped like the ball in Times Square on New Year's Eve. I didn't simply wake one morning having lost the golden horseshoe. No, mine was a slow and painful extraction. The scores in the daily log decreased like the numbers of the pages of a novel when thumbed from back to front: 103 to 51 to 34 to 23, and eventually down to my personal all-time low of 7.

During the twenty-hour stint of dealing with our seventh set, we experienced all of the theatrical effects that accompany the approach, arrival, and departure of a low-pressure system at sea. Early in the set, late in the day, black clouds pushed across the sky, dimming the house lights to that point of near darkness that takes your breath away with anticipation for the start of the performance. There was a relative stillness, a momentary hush.

The first winds from the southeast were playful as they sang. Newly formed white-caps clapped the side of the *Hannah Boden*, keeping time like hands on thighs. The breeze stiffened suddenly, sending the American flag into an awkward syncopation, flapping in the rigging, half a beat ahead of the waves that curled and splashed onto the rail. Heavy drops of spray plopped onto the deck and splatted against bulkheads, sporadic licks of quick-tempoed sticks on a snare drum. Carrying the short chop was a long and deep rolling swell, the kettledrums of the orchestra. Supplying the underlying "thrum," the swells gently lifted and lowered the *Hannah Boden*.

Tension mounted as the wind increased; when it registered 40 knots, a symphony of sound and motion was in full swing. The rhythmical pounding of bow into sea, and a madrigal of wind across and through rigging, was accompanied by the screeching of chain straining against shackle. Another 10 knots of wind, and the "twang" of stay wires moved an octave higher. Waves crashing into and onto the *Hannah Boden* in sync with 70 knots of wind created a throbbing steel vibrato.

When the wind exceeded 70 knots, pandemonium ensued with a violent confusion of sound and motion. Jarring, harsh, and discordant, the nonmusic wore down and discouraged the audience, which was patiently waiting for the conductor to regain control of the elements. The only remaining shred of order was provided by the steady drone of the diesel engines, without which the scene would have been one of total mayhem.

"This sucks" was the simple yet all-encompassing sentiment of the crew as we waited for some semblance of calm to return to our stirred-up world. Steering the boat into the raging sea, I checked the barometer every few minutes, praying for an indication of rising pressure. Atmospheric pressure is a strange thing. The ocean erupting and air churning violently would indicate, to a reasonable person, great pressure, not a lack of it. The situation seems to call for a relief valve to open automatically and let off a bit of steam, stabilizing the elements. But in meteorology, the opposite is true. We were pounded by the waves for hours, waiting for a break, a rising barometer to let the wind out of the storm's sails so we could haul back set number seven.

Bad weather at sea is inconvenient, and severe weather is sheer torture. Even the simplest, most basic activity becomes a major task. Preparing anything more elaborate than a peanut butter sandwich is unheard of; instead we rely on prepackaged, premeasured, and precooked foods. Unfortunately, because our galley doesn't stock anything predigested, use of the head eventually becomes necessary. Using arms and legs as flying buttresses to keep one's backside in contact with the toilet seat is standard procedure; it's like riding a rodeo bull. Mother Nature's sense of humor, coupled with my lack of timing, occasionally turns the head into a shockingly chilly saltwater bidet, truly the only disadvantage I suffer by virtue of being female. In all other aspects of fishing, I consider myself on a level playing field with my male co-workers. We all achieved identical marks in misery. No one was cheated.

When the wind switched to northwest and diminished to a steady 40 knots, we located our end beeper and commenced haulback. The seas had settled into a fierce rhythm; together with the relentless 40 knots of wind, they performed one last number, far from melodious. More of a march or a dirge, the song was a broken record that played over and over for days.

By set number ten, the men had had enough. I suspect that their pride and their respect for me as captain is all that kept them from asking me to take them home. Their inclination to head for the barn was clear to me, although disguised as well-intentioned advice. Their hints were less than subtle. Remarks ranging from helpful suggestions about the merit of beating the rest of the fleet to the dock to receive the highest price, to heartfelt concern for the quality and freshness of our first day's catch, were plentiful. Although we had a good trip aboard, it wasn't enough. We needed to fill the hold. The crew always wants to go home; it's a fact of fishing. I was unwilling to allow them to distract me from my goal. If the fishing had remained as good as it had been for the first five sets, we would surely have been on our way to Gloucester by this point, but it didn't, so we weren't.

The previous few days had been marked not by the number of fish that were lowered into the hold but by the boats that left the grounds for the dock. Our eighth set said good-bye to the *Sea Lion VIII*. L.T. and his crew were steaming happily toward Portland, Maine, with a hold full of fish and a rumored high price. Next to leave, also bound for Portland, was the *Stephanie Vaughn*. Her men had made nineteen consecutive sets, an amazing feat, and were relieved to have passed the test of endurance. While making set number ten, we waved farewell to the *Eagle Eye*. John had managed to top off his fish hold in the berth east of me, successfully avoiding the sharks that had driven Tommy away. It seemed, at least to my crew, that everyone but us was going home.

Although I have never admitted it, I have often felt a twinge of envy when boats head for the dock after completing their fishing. Now, with the fish growing scarcer with every set and the weather serving up a daily ration of shit, the temptation was great to join the parade of boats steaming west. I could have easily justified going home. After ten sets, we had over 40,000 pounds of swordfish aboard, more than enough for this to be considered a fine trip. However, I knew that Bob Brown would be displeased if I ended the trip after so few sets; that was my strongest reason for staying. My desire to keep the boss happy, and his opinion of me high, was powerful enough to enable me to resist both the flotilla of homeward-bounders and the less-than-subliminal messages from my crew.

Halfway through our twelfth set, I was made aware of a real, and compelling, reason to end our trip. Charlie's health had again taken a turn for the worse. The physical embodiment of the trip itself, Charlie was thriving on the 103-fish day, and as near death as he could be and still continue to breathe on the day the tally fell to a mere 23. Somewhere in the middle of hauling, Ringo mentioned to me that he was concerned about Charlie and that perhaps we should consider taking him ashore. If it had been anyone but Ringo, I would have seen the concern as a ploy to convince me to throw in the towel. I had noticed that Charlie had grown thinner and paler each day since set five, but attributed his appearance to the wretched weather and sleep deprivation.

Not wanting to shrug Ringo off, I agreed to check on Charlie, who was back aft in the cart house as usual. Ringo hauled while I visited the stern. The sight of Charlie immediately saddened me. Curled up in a fetal position and lying on a covered hook box, Charlie slept while Peter coiled every leader that slid down the clothesline. Like the parent of a sleeping child, Peter motioned to me please not to wake his shipmate. When Ringo backed the boat down for a fish, I pulled Peter from the cart house onto the main deck, where we could talk without disturbing our sick friend.

"How long has he been unable to work?" I asked.

"This is the third day. He tries, but he's just

too weak. It's okay; I can keep up with the gear," Peter answered proudly.

"Yes, I can see that. But I'm planning to fish another five or six nights, and we're six days from the dock. What kind of shape will he be in twelve days from now? I can send him in with the next boat heading that way, or we can leave as soon as we finish hauling today."

"We're all anxious to go home, as you know. But Charlie won't want to be the reason for you to cut the trip short."

"I will leave that decision for him to make; it's his health. Send him forward to see me when he wakes." I returned to the hauling station to relieve Ringo. As Peter hustled back to the cart house to continue doing the work of two men, I realized how lucky I was to have him aboard. I wondered what to do. Although the decision when to go home is ultimately mine to make, if any member of the crew demands to be taken ashore, it is my legal obligation to do so. In light of the fact that Charlie had been hiding from me the extent of his sickness, I was sure that Peter was correct. Charlie would insist that he was fine and that I should complete every set needed. My responsibilities as captain include the well-being of the crew as well as the prosperity of the trip. I needed to balance one against the other and come to a decision. Some years ago, I had faced a similar situation and made the wrong decision. The result of my bad decision is the single most excruciating memory of my life.

A young and rather inexperienced captain, I was eager to prove myself a moneymaker. Steaming to the Grand Banks from Maine on my first boat, the *Gloria Dawn*, I carried a crew that included the infamous Uncle Patty. Having made his acquaintance days before by pulling him out of an ice-cold Portland Harbor and a drunken stupor, as described near the start of this book, I now had to decide what to do with this latest addition to my crew who was suffering horribly from alcohol withdrawal.

Despite Uncle Patty's wild hallucinations and conversations with late family members spoken in Gaelic, a language he didn't know, I took the advice of the rest of the crew and stayed on course for the fishing grounds. "He'll be fine," his friends assured me. "He'll come out of it soon. He always has." And they were right. Patty's physical thrashings ceased, his nonsensical babbling ended, and he no longer had to be restrained from trying to jump overboard. Patty's "rum horrors" finally subsided when he died in his bunk the morning that we were to make our first set of the trip. Clearly, I should have headed back the minute Patty started babbling.

My first experience handling a dead body was as unpleasant as it is unforgettable. Both the Canadian and the U.S. Coast Guards refused to come offshore and take the body off our hands, teaching me a hard lesson. When it comes to dead bodies, one should always lie to the Coast Guard and report the condition as a possible coma, no matter how stiff and yellow the corpse. With that lesson learned, I faced the problem of what to do with the body.

I remember thinking that the choices were few and unattractive: a burial at sea (throw him overboard); or cold storage until we reached port (put him in the bait freezer). Imagining the body being torn to pieces by sharks and the severed parts being devoured by crabs and sea fleas, I opted for storage in the boat's bait freezer. Preparing Patty for a ride in the freezer is what stays with me most vividly today. Several attempts to close Patty's eyes were futile; his lids refused to stay shut and popped open like spring-loaded window shades, revealing a haunting blue stare. A sleeping bag pulled down over his head and tied around his ankles like he was a sack of potatoes was all we had to insulate ourselves from the dead man's trance and render the situation a tad less creepy. Patty was lowered into the freezer, where he lay on top of thousands of frozen bait fish, giving the expression "dead as a mackerel" real meaning.

It was the trip that wasn't. We never got the opportunity to get the first hook wet; we had to head home to Portland to unload Patty from the freezer. During the voyage home, we encountered the most severe and long-lasting winter storm of my fishing career. For days I wondered if Patty's eyes were still open.

As we hauled the gear aboard the *Hannah Boden*, I waited for Charlie to come forward to talk with me. Briefly, I considered the odds that Charlie might end up in the bait freezer before our arrival in Gloucester, and quickly shook the image from my head, whispering to myself, "He's just seasick."

When the time came to get the bait out to thaw for the night's set, Ringo caught my attention. With a hand on the bait freezer's door latch, he raised one eyebrow in question. Before I could explain that I wanted to talk with Charlie before making any decision about whether to set or not, Charlie was behind me at the rail, asking what I wanted of him. Pulling the clutch control into neutral, and stopping the drum from turning, I sat on the rail to take a good look at Charlie. His face was gaunt and his oil clothes hung from his frail frame like a suit from a wire hanger. With the exception of Peter, who remained in the stern coiling briskly, the crew gathered around to hear the conversation. "Do you want to head for the dock, Charlie?" I asked point-blank.

"Yes, doesn't everyone? Are you taking a poll or something? Since when does the captain ask the crew when to—"

I interrupted Charlie mid-sentence. "Since you don't look too good, Charlie. Since I'm worried about your health. I'm not asking the crew, I'm asking you. Are you physically up to finishing the trip, say, five or six more sets?"

Charlie had to have felt the pressure from his shipmates. Although they remained silent, their eyes showed a glimmer of hope that this might be the last haulback. Charlie had the power to terminate the trip. All he had to do was ask me to take him ashore. There would be no shame in returning to port with over 40,000 pounds after only twelve sets. Charlie scanned the faces of his fellow crew, took a long thoughtful look at me and then at the deck, and then answered soberly. "I am truly sick. I don't know what's wrong with me, but please don't use me as an excuse to go home. I don't want to be responsible for the size of the paychecks. Hell, I have two daughters to support." Charlie shifted his stare from the deck to the long faces of Kenny and Carl. "Sorry, guys. The captain intends to fill the hold, and I'm not going to stand in her way." Now the ball was back in my court.

Ringo was still holding the freezer door, with the same question mark on his face. I nodded to him. He yelled to the others, "Give me a hand with the bait. Let's go!" Kenny and Carl shuffled over to help with the bait that they would have preferred stay in the freezer until the next trip. Ringo, who rarely missed an opportunity to torment the younger men, tossed a 40-pound box to Carl and teased, "Hey, snot-nose, five or six more sets... Jesus, by the time we get to Gloucester, you'll be old enough to have a legal drink!"

As the box hit Carl in the chest, he snarled back, "Fuck you, Grandpa!" I laughed from my seat on the rail. Thinking back, I can't say whether I was relieved or disappointed that Charlie was willing to persevere, allowing me the chance to load the boat. I laughed alone until the boat lurched to starboard. A wave caught the side of the hull full-force, slamming the steel and sending into the air a sheet of water that landed squarely on the back of my neck and cascaded down my collar. Gallons of water gushed into my overalls, ballooning my pants out into an obese shape. Rivers flowed the length of my legs, filling my boots to capacity. As the overflow trickled onto the deck, the pants deflated.

Drenched from head to toe, I muttered "Son of a bitch" as I pulled off my boots, poured them out, and jammed them back on over sopping-wet socks. Now the only long face belonged to me; the crew cracked up. Ringo slammed the bait freezer closed, the men returned to their usual positions, and off we went, rolling and pounding along the string of gear, stopping only occasionally for a fish. I wondered what I had done to deserve this mistreatment, what I could do to rectify the situation, and who had gained the golden horseshoe that fate had snatched away from me.

Cold and tired, I recorded 2,000 pounds at the end of the day and wondered whether I had done the right thing by preparing to set in the same spot again. By eleven that night, the

40-mile string was again behind us, and I was still wondering. If the lucky number seven had been bad, what would the ominous number thirteen have in store for us? I spent three hours in my bunk that night not sleeping. The northeast wind had increased to a nasty 50 knots. The bow of the *Hannah Boden* dove into a trough, and my bunk fell out from under me. I hung in midair until the bow climbed the next crest, bringing my mattress back to meet me with the force of a linebacker. "Jesus!" I yelled. "I have just about had it with this happy horseshit. Will this wind ever stop blowing?"

My answer came from the wheelhouse, where Kenny was jogging the boat back to our east end. "It don't look good, Ma. The last map shows a newly formed low just south of us. Should be a fun day."

"Great."

The first light of day, cast down from a sky in motion, was bright white. White curls and cresting waves, white streaks and puddles of foam, and white clouds of spray greeted our white-knuckled grips, which held tightly anything unmoving that might keep us upright. Within an hour, all eyes and mouths were ringed with white, crusty, salty deposits left behind by the wind-driven mist.

The mainline hung between crests like a tightrope, the motion of the waves spinning and twisting leaders and ball-drops into hopeless springs that met with steel blades to separate them from the line before entering the

259

block. I cut, and cut, and cut—hundreds of snarled leaders. Wind and sea pushed the *Hannah Boden* down the string of gear faster than the line could be spooled onto the drum. As I reversed the engine, backing the boat into the sea to haul the loop of slack line trailing behind us, a wall of water climbed over the stern and rushed the length of the deck. Up to my waist in water, I held on to the rail to keep from being swept away from the controls, and watched helplessly as Kenny washed around the deck, never releasing the swordfish he rode like an inflatable water toy. Finally the water exited the deck through the scuppers, and I counted crew. Peter poked a dripping head around the corner of the cart house and flashed me an "okay" sign. The other men slowly emerged from various corners of the deck and scurried back to their positions.

Ringo caught my eye. Pointing at the bait freezer, he waited for my response. I glanced at the bulkhead to check the fish tally. Four sections had been hauled for three sickly-looking swordfish. Suddenly, a queer wave slammed the starboard quarter, throwing what felt like a ton of bricks onto me, buckling my legs. When I regained my posture and my visibility, Ringo was still waiting for an answer about bait. I gritted my teeth and shook my head no. No, we would not set tonight. Set number thirteen was taking its toll in gear and the clock. I realized that by the time we finished hauling, we would have too few leaders and too little time to try again tonight.

It was a dreadfully long day. At dusk, I could finally see the last beeper ahead of the bow. The end was in sight, and I was more than relieved. The day had been a total bust, seven ratty swordfish that would not begin to pay for the bait it had taken to catch them, to say nothing of the lightsticks, mono, and fuel. Ringo summed up the day with a smile: "We didn't catch many, but they sure were small."

Discouraged with the fishing, and frustrated with the weather conditions, the men secured the deck and climbed into their bunks for their first good night's rest in two weeks. I knew what they were thinking as they drifted off to sleep, because I had had the same thoughts many times when I worked as a deckhand aboard the *Walter Leeman*. They were thinking that they had come to sea to make a living, not to live, and that in the future they would be careful to sign on with a captain who *does* have a life other than fishing. They were thinking, hopefully, that perhaps the idiot in the wheelhouse had finally had a vision of homecoming. They were reasoning, and rightfully so, that the northeast wind on the stern quarter indicated travel in the direction of the dock. They were thinking that in six days they might be sitting on dry and unmoving bar stools, sipping cold beers, telling stories, and receiving congratulations for another successful trip. The notion of making just one more set, unbearable except in the mind of the captain, was simply unthinkable.

The unbearable and unthinkable became tolerable and probable when I said to Ringo, who had stood the only watch during the night, relieving me for five wonderful hours of sleep, "Please wake the men, and get bait out for tonight's set."

"You're kidding. The guys assumed we were on our way home! Jesus...you won't make many friends today."

"I never said we were done fishing. And besides, I'm here to make money, not friends." The five hours had done little to restore my usual good nature.

"Yeah, me, too. I'm here to make money so that I can make friends with the IRS when we go in. When do you think that might be? How many more sets are you planning to make?"

"I'm planning to fill the hold, however many sets it takes. It will take more than one bad set and a little foul weather to drive me away. We only need another six or seven thousand pounds."

Ringo nodded and descended the stairs to wake his shipmates, their worst nightmare come true. Partway down the stairs, as an afterthought, Ringo added, "That's why you're on the pointy end." And he was right. Making unpopular decisions is part of being the captain.

I remembered the many lectures Alden gave me when he offered me my first job as captain. At the time, I considered Alden excessive, his attitude harsh. Among other things, Alden explained that fishing boats are not run by a democratic form of government and that I should *never* listen to *anything* the crew suggests. "The main difference between captain and crew is," Alden explained, "the crew always wants to go home and the captain is the one asshole who wants to stay." Alden was right about a lot of things. Now that I was "the one asshole who wants to stay," I thought back to when I'd been one of those who desperately wanted to go home, and how much I'd disliked Alden when he said "Get the bait out." I could certainly empathize with what my crew must have been feeling as Ringo relayed the message that would distance them from me and make me the enemy in their minds.

As the day progressed, the weather improved; it actually got nice. The wind that had been howling for days managed a few dying gasps in early afternoon before running entirely out of breath. The sun peeked out and shimmered on the last of the lazy whitecaps to unfurl. Now that the weather was silent, the only noise aboard the *Hannah Boden* was man-made. From the wheelhouse I could hear the sounds of discontent: bickering, pouting, whining, and the frequent slamming of refrigerator and stateroom doors by disgruntled deckhands. Although I found it impossible to ignore the commotion from below, it would not provoke a response. As of yet, there was no call for a fire ax to penetrate the television screen. Perhaps I had finally outgrown my temper.

All eyes avoided contact with mine when I ventured below to flush the men out onto

263

the deck, to prepare our fourteenth set. Conversation hushed upon my entrance into the galley; the crew was suddenly engrossed in their hundredth viewing of *Lonesome Dove*. I was happy to see Charlie at the table, nibbling some crackers. The calming of the sea had settled his stomach, which had been heaving with, and into, the ocean. "Time to set out, guys. Let's go!" My enthusiasm, which is usually contagious, was unable to penetrate the somber atmosphere.

The beeper beginning set fourteen splashed into the ocean at 45° 45' N and 46° 50' W; this was 180 miles southwest of where we had made our first thirteen sets. The previous day's storm had succeeded in jumbling up the fleet. A new lineup had been organized. Tommy and George had managed to screw themselves entirely out of the picture by setting all over one another the night preceding the gale. They had spent the last forty-eight hours untangling their combined 80-mile mess. The tide had swept the two boats, and corresponding wads of gear, east of the rest of us like one giant raft of flotsam.

This section of the break on which we set ran north and south. I drove the boat to the south, in and out of telltale schools of bait and flocks of birds, thinking, but not daring to say, This looks good. Looking down onto the deck, I watched Ringo as he stared into the water rushing by the side of the hull. Ringo seemed in deep concentration. I wondered what he found so thought-provoking. Never a com-

264

plainer, Ringo wasn't one to whine that he wanted to go home, although he surely must have.

I imagined that Ringo might be thinking about the Internal Revenue Service, with whom he had been trying to get square for four months. At the end of each trip, when the paychecks from the previous trip were handed out, Ringo had taken his pay to the local IRS office, where the lion's share went toward his debt to the U.S. government. Ringo was far from alone in his trouble with the IRS. A large percentage of commercial fishermen, including myself, have fallen behind with income taxes at one time or another. The reason is clear. No taxes are withheld from paychecks. Deckhands are responsible for keeping records, filing, and paying in one lump sum what is owed at the end of the fiscal year. Why the U.S. government would trust a bunch of saltwater Gypsies with this responsibility is beyond my comprehension; some fishermen I know have never even filed. Many have no bank accounts for the IRS to attach and can store everything they own in one 30-gallon garbage bag.

Ringo looked up and caught me watching him. Stretching his arms straight out from his sides, he yelled to me, "Hey, Ma. Why don't you catch all you need tonight? Some of us are ready to go home!"

Sticking my head out the window, I yelled back, "No shit!" Ringo smiled and vanished behind the cart house dragging a tray of bait behind him. I went back to concentrating on the set. Once the gear was in the water, the guys cleaned and arranged the deck for the haulback, then hit their bunks without so much as a good-night. While the crew slept, I steamed the boat. Scanning the surface with the searchlight for birds and bait, and finding plenty of both, I was as excited as I had been fourteen nights before, after making the first set of the trip. The only problem I anticipated was the mood of the crew. I had to deal with these men until we returned to the dock in Gloucester, whenever that might be, and hoped for things to return to pleasant.

My apprehension was alleviated when the lower lips that had protruded into pouts had been sucked back into place; some even turned into faint grins when they joined me on the deck at three forty-five A.M. to begin haulback. The men had apparently left all melancholia behind in their bunks and were resigned to the idea that they were indeed stuck with me for the duration. They would make the best of it. The morning couldn't have been more beautiful. Two sections into the haul, the men were fully back to their good-natured selves, teasing and tormenting one another in their usual fashion. Fish were coming aboard at a steady clip, which might have had something to do with the recovering morale.

It was a nice run of fish, short and stocky, mostly markers that would fill the hold in a hurry. At the halfway point, with twenty-six fish tallied, I stood over the fish hold hatch and looked down, remarking that the empty cavity had grown quite small. "Wow! Another four thousand pounds and we'll be out of here."

"Why don't you pull one last rabbit out of your hat, and we'll leave today?" Ringo suggested.

"If the tally hits seventy fish for the day, we'll do just that," I answered. "But if it's anything short of the seventy mark, we'll have to try again. I guess we should get the bait out now." I could feel the men's hearts sink with the mention of another set, but they kept their chins up while they pulled the bait out of the freezer for the set they would hate to make, and we anxiously started on the second half of the gear.

Doubleheaders and flurries of fat fish were met with cheers from the crew, followed by an empty half a section, met by despondence. The last three sections of gear took the men and me on a classic emotional roller coaster ride. Each time I backed the boat, three or four fish would land on the deck, and then there would be nothing, then another three-fish flurry, followed by many slack leaders.

When fish number 70 slapped the deck, it landed with such force it sounded like a cannon. I wailed, "Ouch! Jesus Christ Almighty!" The men didn't know which way to turn. Here on deck was their ticket west, a cause for jubilation, but I appeared to have been injured, a cause for concern. My fists and eyes both clamped shut, I gritted my teeth and groaned loudly in pain, then there was silence.

I could sense my crew around me, and could see their worried faces through my clenched eyelids.

Carl's voice broke the silence. He asked with trepidation, "What happened, Ma? Are you all right?"

I took a pained breath before speaking. "It's that goddamned horseshoe..." I opened my eyes and smiled, "...returned to its rightful owner."

12

MUG-UP

Three crew members and I watched with interest as a fourth man extracted his own tooth with a pair of needle-nosed pliers. We were catching fish and could not afford to steam the 600 miles to Newfoundland and the closest dentist, or risk losing this productive berth to the boat next door. Even the man, who had been in agony for days before finally ripping roots from gum, never asked to be taken ashore, never considered interrupting the trip for something as minor as an abscessed tooth. Emergency dental work is common among longliners and other fishermen who spend months at sea. The legendary Charlie Johnson once filed off smooth what was left of his two front teeth after being hit in the mouth with a leaded swivel, and fished on as if it never happened. And Alden Leeman used Elmer's Glue to hold a temperamental crown in place for three months before he found the time to visit his dentist. Shipboard dental care is just one example of the perseverance embodied by offshore fishermen and the tunnel vision that develops when in pursuit of fish and paychecks.

Tunnel vision is a symptom of the blinding determination we all share while at sea. At the far end of the tunnel is a boat loaded with fish, and we do whatever is necessary to reach that end. Whether the obstacle is physical, emotional, or mechanical, it will be overcome. Mechanical breakdowns are most common, and often tax the ingenuity of even the most adroit tinkerer. The jury-riggings and contraptions born at sea are akin to the most complex gadgets one can imagine. When faced with mechanical problems, fishermen are quite imaginative and can almost always piece together something that will get us through the trip using duct tape, hose clamps, and a tube of marine sealant. Most fishing vessels have large storage compartments overflowing with nuts, bolts, and a variety of spare parts. Even broken items are saved when replaced in case they can be used in some other way later. Almost nothing is discarded as useless.

On one trip aboard the *Gloria Dawn*, I caught in a 5-gallon bucket what was leaking from the main engine's coolant circulating pump and pumped it back into the expansion tank through a length of garden hose using a bilge pump rigged with an automatic float switch. At the same time, my 12-volt alternator shit the bed, necessitating that I steal 12 volts of current from the 32-volt bank of batteries; some makeshift jumper cables did the trick. Later in the same trip, the hydraulic steering stopped functioning. We rigged a fairly crude mechanical steering system with a series of lines, pulleys, and a block and tackle. When we returned to Portland, the boss was more impressed that we were able to complete the trip in the face of so many malfunctions than he was disappointed with how few fish we had caught.

Often, good ol' Yankee ingenuity comes into play in the galley. Talented cooks are resourceful in preparing meals without certain key ingredients in less-than-ideal conditions. Years ago, aboard the *Walter Leeman*, the electric heating element in the oven burned out early in the trip. With no oven, there was no roasting, baking, or broiling, leaving only boiling and frying as possible cooking methods. Frying is not commonly done aboard a boat for obvious reasons: hot fat and rolling seas. Basically, I boiled everything, every meal, even a turkey. The very next trip, with a new element in place, we sailed with no eggs. I had neglected to put them on the grocery list. Preparing breakfast for six hungry fishermen for thirty consecutive mornings with no eggs took some innovation on my part; as I recall, it was the last trip on which I was asked to cook.

The most valuable men aboard a fishing boat are those who can successfully wear the blinders, who can see the light at the end of the tunnel, no matter how dim, and who can be most imaginative when dealing with the obstacles that threaten to pull the shade. The most sought-after crew members are the men who do not question whether something can be repaired, but instead offer suggestions, no matter how outlandish, on how to fix what is broken. The most amazing display of blinding determination I have ever witnessed was when Bob Brown attempted to propel the *Hannah Boden*, whose engine had quit at sea, using two small tarpaulins as sails. His motive was to avoid an expensive commercial tow.

Determination, perseverance, and resourcefulness are hard qualities for a captain to measure in prospective crew members while hiring at the dock. These attributes don't come to light until needed; this is what makes hiring a green guy risky. In my experience, very few men are willing to pull their own teeth.

12 + 1

WEST BOUND

"Home" always sounds funny to me when I say it in reference to Gloucester. Gloucester is where we unload the catch, receive paychecks, and re-outfit for another month at sea. It has never felt like home to me. My home is Isle Au Haut. I have family on the island. My grandmother is buried there, on top of the hill where the barn used to be, and her parents, too. I suppose I will someday rest there under the blanket of moss, surrounded by salt air and the remains of a white picket fence.

There would be no time for a visit to Isle Au Haut this month. I would stay aboard the *Hannah Boden*, tied to the dock, and help Bob Brown turn the boat around for the October moon, our final trip of this year's Grand Banks season. For ten years I had spent far more days at sea than on the island. I now had the sense that I was leaving, rather than returning to, my place of comfort. I felt no great sadness in parting company with the Banks of Newfoundland, but experienced the excitement of leaving home for the first time, filled with anticipation. The price of fish was what the six of us would fret over for the next five days, the last of the "make-or-breaks" that would determine the financial success of the trip.

The *Hannah Boden* was bustling with activity the first full day of westward travel. The weather was calm, allowing the men to begin the extensive scrubbing of every inch of the 100-foot steel boat. Even Charlie perked up a bit, doing what he could to help clean what endless days and nights of fishing had produced. I watched from the bridge as the crew disassembled beeper buoys, rinsed them with fresh water, and stowed them forward. Five hundred bullet floats disappeared into a storage compartment, along with gaffs, meat hooks, knives, and fishing gear. The crew must have known I was watching; four of the men, as if on cue, each armed with a gaff at the starboard rail, pulled the long poles in a rowing motion through the water, pretending to propel the *Hannah Boden* toward home. Opening the window to acknowledge the effort, I yelled "Faster!" Gloucester, just by dint of being made of solid earth, was considered home by the crew; they were happy to be moving in that direction. Reaching port with a full fish hold was the best of all possible outcomes. The crew and I shared responsibility for the trip. They were proud of the accomplishment and fully deserving of the good spirits they would enjoy all the way to the dock.

The first two nights of steaming, I had no contact with Bob Brown. He was away from home and the radio. I was anxious to hear from him, to share our excitement and give him enough advance notice of our arrival in Gloucester to enable him to make the necessary arrangements. He would be thrilled, I imagined, to learn that we were once again on our way with a boatload of swordfish. A trip such as this would not only be a financial victory, but also reflected well the hard work of the boat's owner and his ability to manage and maintain a successful fishing operation. Bob would be proud of us, I thought.

During the daylight hours, I rarely saw a man without a scrub brush, deck broom, or gallon of bleach in hand. The list of chores was lengthy and detailed, and the crew enthusiastically crossed out items; each chore completed, that many more miles of ocean astern of us. As the dried bloodstains, bait juice, and fish slime dissolved under the stiff-bristled brushes, the pages of my notebook filled with mock settlement sheets. Three days into the steam, I had worked every angle, playing with various prices and total weights, to answer the most prominent question in our collective head: "How much money will we make this trip?"

Early in our third night, with the radio's volume turned up so as not to miss Bob's call, I marked our position on the chart, 43° 58' N and 55° 15' W. All fish reports from the Banks were grim, the boats remaining to our

274

east now suffering the dreaded dark side of the moon. No one had left the grounds since we had, and I hoped the reports of poor fishing would increase the price of fish. Labor Day had come and gone; with its passage went the $4 per pound we had received in both July and August. Many of New England's resorts and restaurants are seasonal, as are backyard charcoal grills; September brings a drop in the local demand for swordfish and the price goes down accordingly. I hoped we would average over $3, and grabbed my notebook and calculator to grope the numbers once again and relieve the knot in my stomach that had formed from worry. Finally, Bob's voice boomed through the speakers. "WQX six four seven to the *Hannah Boden*. Are you on here, Linda?"

I sprang from the chair, startled. Tossing notebook, pen, and calculator onto the chart table, I dove for the mike. "Whiskey Romeo Charlie five two four five. Hi, Bob! Over." I could hear the excitement in my own voice, and took a deep breath to suppress my childish urge to blurt out the good news. I didn't want to sound like I was bragging. I thought Bob's next transmission would never end. He told me all about his last two days and how glad he was to be home again. He spoke of uncomfortable heat, hotel rooms, and traffic jams until I thought I would explode. I fidgeted, shifting my weight from foot to foot until his train of thought finally came around to his boat, the fishing, and me.

"Gee, last time we spoke you had just had a seven-fish day and were relocating. You must be in the middle of a set now. How is everything going? Did you get back on the fish? Over."

I loved being the bearer of good news. I attempted and failed to sound nonchalant. "We're on the fifty-five west line, and heading for the barn. We'll be at the dock Saturday night. We had seventy-five fish our last set. We're full! Over." I waited for Bob's reaction, some congratulations, a verbal pat on the back, a heartfelt "That-a-girl!" But instead there was a long pause filled with static. I played with the squelch control, adjusting the knob to bring Bob's voice closer and clearer. His next transmission hit me like a rogue wave.

Bob's voice was more than disappointed, it was angry. "You left a seventy-fish set? You're joking! Linda, we discussed this the very morning you left Gloucester. You have a good set, and you leave it to come home...unbelievable..."

I answered feebly, "But the hold is full. Over." I wasn't able to launch a well-reasoned argument including price and timing for our next trip. My hyperextended perseverance had been wrenched out of joint. This was certainly not the conversation I had envisioned.

"Well, it's too late to argue about it now. You must be four hundred miles away from the fish." Bob's tone had lightened up a bit, perhaps sensing that he had devastated me.

"I'll make the arrangements to unload you at four o'clock Sunday morning. Do not come in Saturday night. Wait until it's time to unload. We don't want the men to disappear or get drunk before the work is done. Over."

"Roger. Over." My voice flattened under the weight of my boss's criticism.

"I'll talk with you tomorrow night and you can give me your list of repairs needed and your gear order for next trip. Over."

"Roger. Over."

"Have a safe night. Give my best to the crew. See you later. WQX six four seven, clear with the *Hannah Boden*."

" 'Bye." I knew I hadn't heard the end of Bob's disapproval of my decision to head to shore. Sitting back in the captain's chair, I stared into the radar screen, hypnotized by the sweep into a trancelike state in which I contemplated my love/hate relationship with my boss. At this moment, the hating part came easy, the love was harder. Fishing was simple, relationships complicated, I thought. I had learned long ago that any decision that pleased the crew would displease the owner and vice versa. Bob would have been delighted if I had reported both fish hold and bait freezer full of fish and that we were now attempting to fill our bunks. In fact, Bob probably would have suggested packing a few under the galley table. The crew, of course, would have been planning a mutiny. Yes, I had admiration and respect for the toughest man and most savvy fisherman I had ever met, but hated his ability to make me feel two inches tall. I should have been overjoyed to be steaming west, but after talking with Bob, would have preferred to remain at sea.

I didn't actually love Bob Brown, I mused. What I did love was the knowledge that there existed a man like him. If Bob were in my shoes, he certainly would have stayed and fished on, despite all of the logical reasons to go home. Price, quality, crew, and full hold be damned, Bob would have stayed simply because he was slaying the fish, the consummate fisherman, a purist. I liked Bob most, I thought, when times were bad. Poor fishing and slight paychecks sent the crew scurrying from the *Hannah Boden*, leaving Bob and me alone to wade through the bilge. Bob had instilled in me the value of loyalty by standing by me during long winters of short paychecks, saying, "We work on a share basis. We share the good, and we share the bad. Right now, we're sharing the bad."

I lay awake in my bunk for hours that night, despising Bob Brown and contemplating my greeting for him when he met us on the dock to catch the lines. I imagined that I would tell him to shove his beloved boat up his ass, as Ringo would say, "stern first!" I'd had the very same thought in the past, and fortunately had never verbalized it. If I had known then what I know now, I would have spent less energy hating Bob for pushing me beyond myself and more time learning what he had to teach me about persistence and determination.

I would have further exploited his vast maritime knowledge.

On our fourth day of traveling west from the Grand Banks, I certainly didn't spend any time thinking that I might someday miss Bob Brown. My immediate concern was the price of fish. Prolonged meditations on the size of our probable paychecks, briefly interrupted by contemplation of the concept of "home," occupied my mind.

I wondered, on our fourth night, while passing south of Sable Island, if ghosts had the emotional capacity for envy. Many souls of seamen lingering in the Graveyard of the North Atlantic might resent this elated crew and captain's journey home. How many ghosts of men residing here were once in our exact situation, happily returning to port, triumphant, laden with fish, desperate to see the first lights through the windows of kitchens and bedrooms in the homes along the shores of Cape Ann? Pining away for wives and lovers, the men must surely have felt twinges of excitement in both hearts and groins for what their lives had been lacking during their days and nights at sea. Then, without warning, some disaster had struck, foiling all anticipated unions, plans for reunion, and indeed ending life itself.

"Creepy, ain't it?" Carl asked, his voice just above a whisper, as he gazed out the starboard window toward Sable Island, his eyes as black as the night.

"You read my mind. I was just thinking

about all the fishermen who never made it home. This area is a friggin' death trap. The loss of the guys with the *Andrea Gail* was an eyeopener. It can happen to anyone. It could happen to us."

"Yeah. That would suck."

I envied Carl's youthful ability to keep the conversation from getting too deep, and realized that I would have answered Alden in the same way when I was nineteen and on my way home after thirty days at sea. Until October 1991, when the Halloween gale took the lives of comrades, shipwrecks were just one form of sea story; the possibility of being personally involved seemed remote. It couldn't happen to me. Some would call it denial, but I always preferred to think of my attitude as a way of coping with the reality that I had chosen a dangerous life.

Readers of *The Perfect Storm* are curious about my experience in the Halloween gale, and are often disappointed when I explain to them that where I was located the weather was not life-threatening. This is not to downplay the severity of the storm. I knew how bad it was when I saw the wreckage it left in its wake. I lost six friends in that storm. But I was 600 miles east of where the *Andrea Gail* is believed to have gone down, and 400 miles east of where the 100-foot waves were recorded.

I would be lying if I said that my crew and I were never concerned for our own safety during that storm. We were in radio contact with the men west of us whose lives were in danger, and something in their voices scared us deeply. Fortunately for us, though, by the time the storm reached our position, it had diminished to a state somewhat less than perfect. We encountered 70 knots of wind for two days; this was truly miserable, but by no means the worst winds we had ever seen.

Although no one had been seriously injured this season aboard the *Hannah Boden*, we all understood too well the dangers inherent to commercial fishing, regarded by many as the most dangerous profession. I thought that being washed overboard and swallowed up by the sea would be the easiest way to go, if a salty death should be in my future. I would much prefer that end to some I know of. We had all seen or heard about grisly, grotesque, and not-so-freak shipboard accidents.

Perhaps the most lethal weapon aboard a longliner is the hook. Both size and sharpness render hooks unforgiving when they decide to dive into and tear through flesh. Not as common, but certainly not unusual, are wounds caused by shark bites. The jaws of a Mako shark are like the proverbial steel trap; in an instant they can latch onto the calf of one whose back is turned. Rows of razor-sharp teeth puncture oil pants, boots, skin, and flesh, and sink into solid bone like nails into balsa wood. Then there are the accidents that occur on slippery decks of stern-trawlers in bad weather. The rocking and rolling motion can pitch an off guard and fatigued man into the massive moving parts of deck equipment, severing limbs like dry twigs. Less ghastly, but just as fatal, are the internal injuries that result from being crushed under the weight of a rogue wave. We had been lucky in so many ways this season. None of us aboard the *Hannah Boden* had suffered anything more than a nasty gash with a rusted knife.

Ringo joined Carl and me on the bridge, and the three of us stared into the night in silence, lost in our own thoughts. The darkness was a shade blacker than the night before. Another twenty-four hours shaved from the waning moon left a thin almond-colored crescent too dim to cast even a single sparkle onto the inkwell of ocean. The steel hull barely disturbed the ebony puddle as she glided quietly through. Like pulling an index finger through a spill of black paint, the boat left a trough of wake that filled in closely behind us, leaving no sign of our passing. As if our thoughts were too intense, Carl broke the silence with a lighthearted inquiry directed at Ringo. "So, what are you going to do when we get ashore?"

"Get drunk and get laid. In that order."

"How about you, Ma? Are you going to get laid while we're in?" Carl asked.

"Is that any kind of question to ask of someone whom you refer to as 'Ma'?" I laughed.

"Well, just curious. So?"

"That's none of your damn business." The truth was, I wouldn't leave the boat long enough to engage in anything of the sort, and the fact that I didn't care bothered me far more than the abstinence itself.

Ringo pushed me out of Carl's line of fire by verbalizing what we certainly all feared but had not spoken. "Getting laid will be nice, but we'll probably all feel like we've been screwed when we hear the price of fish." Here began another conversation about pounds, price, and paychecks, topics I much preferred to any discussion of my sex life. Pounding the keys of my calculator, we massaged the familiar figures once again, pushing variables through the equation to get both best and worst scenarios.

It seems odd that I have always thought of myself as the master of my own destiny when so much of my life has been dictated by forces beyond my control. Man has his hands full predicting the weather, let alone trying to pull the strings that create it. I hadn't yet learned to coerce unwilling fish onto my hooks or stop the moon in its fullest phase until the boat was loaded to the hatch cover. Alden felt this inadequacy when pitted against nature, too, and often quoted, "Tide and time wait for no man, and damn few women!" To me, it was not nature but price that was the most frustrating of all elements of fishing over which I had no control. We had survived the weather and killed plenty of fish; now we had to wait and hope.

My calculations showed that a $1 difference in the price per pound could mean up to a $5,000 difference in the paychecks of the crew—and a possible $10,000 difference in mine. If the price were to fall into the $2 range, which it often does near the end of the season, the crew and I would have little to show for our efforts; anything below a $2 average would result in a broker. We prayed, because praying was all we could do at that point, for an average of better than $3 per pound of swordfish. The numbers, well worthy of worry, cinched the knot in my stomach a little tighter.

Alden once told me that his father, also a fisherman, told him that anyone who chooses to make fishing his occupation solely for the money is in the wrong business. If no thrill is experienced in catching fish, no satisfaction in going to sea and returning to shore, no pride in exclaiming "I am a fisherman," then a life on the water will be unfulfilling, perhaps even unbearable. Among the unhappy with whom I am acquainted, perhaps the most miserable people are those who fish out of necessity rather than out of a love of the sea and the seafaring life. I have always maintained that when I no longer feel a thrill, satisfaction, and pride from fishing, I will start a new career.

I counted myself among the extremely fortunate to work with a crew of five fishermen rather than a group of five guys looking for a large paycheck. It was rare to have a crew the caliber of this one; I had suffered through enough trips with lesser men to know and appreciate the difference. Sure, all five had the desire for a whopping paycheck, as I did. Peter and Charlie had families to support, Ringo needed to get square with the IRS, Carl was saving to buy himself an inshore lobster boat, and Kenny would need a nest egg to carry him through a long winter in Newfoundland, where the government had ceased all fishing of cod, the Canadian fisherman's bread and butter. But regardless of the compensation, these men would be at sea again next month, either with me aboard the *Hannah Boden* or with someone else aboard some other sword-boat, because they are fishermen.

The men continued to scrub, sweep, and organize as we steamed south of Cape Sable, the southwest end of Nova Scotia. It was a clear day, and we saw much of Nova Scotia's sword-fishing fleet, some boats hauling longline, while others chased swordfish with harpoon. A tenacious bunch in small, sturdy wooden boats, these Canadian fishermen could travel less than 100 miles from their homes to the fishing grounds of Middle, Emerald, Lahave, and Brown's Banks, over which we now steamed.

With binoculars, I drew in close the silhouette of a man poised with harpoon at the end of a boat's stand. As the striker released the harpoon into the water at his feet, I felt a familiar rush of adrenaline. Memories of harpooning aboard the *Walter Leeman* came

285

vividly. In my mind's eye, I was the helmsman in the crow's nest at the top of the *Walter Leeman*'s mast, carefully steering the boat onto the fish horned out ahead of us. There was deafening silence and strained concentration as we closed in on the dorsal fins of a slammer. Alden was the striker; he waited in the stand with harpoon cocked over his right shoulder like a javelin. The black fins cut through the water closer, closer...finally, Alden would hurl the pole dartfirst into the water. My heart would stop beating with nervous anticipation. Putting the helm hard to starboard, and pulling the engine into neutral, I wouldn't be sure Alden had hit the fish until I heard the snapping shut of the clothespins. The dartline was jerked from the wooden pins, away from the boat and into the water behind the fish that was now diving, leaving behind a pale red, cloudy stream of blood. I would watch as the 100-fathom basket of line uncoiled into the sea and a buoy splashed in behind it, marking the fish that had just been ironed.

Through the binoculars, I watched with envy as the Canadian striker rerigged his pole for another shot. Harpooning is the most exciting and enjoyable method of catching fish. Unfortunately, most of the good harpooning grounds lie within Canadian boundaries, and the superior productivity of the longline fishery is needed to support the larger vessels and their six-man crews. If I were Canadian, I thought, I would spend my days fishing with a harpoon rather than hooks. The harpoon is primitive, the harpoon fisherman among the last of the true hunters. Virtually anyone can be taught to bait a hook, but few possess the skill, concentration, and coordination to iron a free-swimming fish.

"They sticking any?" Ringo asked me.

"Yes." I nodded with the binoculars still pressed to my eyes. "That guy over there just nailed one." Ringo found our position on the chart and commented that with just over 200 miles to go, we would surely be in Gloucester for a wild Saturday night. Placing the binoculars on the chart table, I reached up and pulled the throttle back a few hundred RPMs. "Thanks for reminding me," I said. "Bob doesn't want us at the dock until daylight Sunday morning, so we might as well slow down."

"Oh, come on, Ma! Not again. You're kidding, right?"

"No. I guess Bob hasn't forgotten about Puerto Rico yet. He has forbidden me to come to the dock until it's time to unload the fish."

"Son of a bitch," Ringo mumbled, and he returned to the galley, where he would clean the freezer and refrigerator while formulating a well-reasoned protest. Although emotional, and quite convincing, his request to go into Gloucester on Saturday night against Bob's wishes would be soundly rejected by me. I, too, remembered the scene in San Juan.

It was stifling hot. We tied up to the Pan-American Dock in San Juan Harbor three hours prior to our scheduled time of arrival. I forbade the crew to stray from the dock until the fish were unloaded and the hold sanitized. Fish caught in the Caribbean are taken from the boat and packed into airline containers at the dock, then flown to the States. The catch is unloaded on a precise schedule to insure that the containers not sit on the hot tarmac for any significant amount of time before being forklifted into the belly of the plane. Once unloading begins, the crew must work efficiently to get all the fish aboard the next plane to leave for Boston.

From the air-conditioned office of our ship's agent, I could see the *Hannah Boden*, and the pay phones on the dock around which my crew had gathered. One of the men was pushing coins into a phone. The men meandered back to the boat, and within minutes, a taxi arrived. The driver handed several brown paper bags out through his window to my crew in exchange for a fistful of green bills.

Sometimes fishermen drink to relax and unwind after a long stint at sea. Sometimes they drink to be sociable, sharing a cold beer with buddies at the local bar and telling fish tales. At this particular time in Puerto Rico, they drank to get drunk. Before the first ton of fish had been hoisted from the hold, the crew, in their impaired state, were fighting among themselves. Bitter, personal, verbal attacks, and finally physical skirmishes, interrupted the flow of fish from the boat. Two of my men climbed the ladder to duke it out on deck, where they had each other by the throat, squeezing with intentions to do harm. With some help, I managed to break them apart before they passed out. A captain of another boat stopped by to say hello and was offered a Bacardi and Coke, which he accepted. Before he had finished his cocktail, the same man who had offered and poured the drink offered to smash the same captain's skull with a cinder block. It was a bad scene. The fish missed their scheduled flight, which endeared me to neither the buyers waiting for the fish at Logan Airport nor to Bob Brown, who arrived at the dock midway through the circus. No, we would not go ashore early this trip.

The earliest of dawn's light on that long-awaited Sunday morning gave us our first sighting of dry land in thirty days: Cape Ann, Massachusetts, the home of Gloucester. Stabilizing birds and outriggers were raised in salutation as we entered the harbor. Coils of dock lines were made ready to toss from bow, midship, and stern to the wharf, where Bob Brown stood, waiting to receive and make fast their bitter ends. Before the after springline hit the dock at his feet, Bob yelled through cupped hands, "Good morning, Linda! When do you want to head back out for the next trip?"

"I thought I would go home for a couple of days," I lied. "What's the price of fish?" Just twelve hours prior to our arrival at the dock, the last leg of our trip had carried the *Hannah Boden* through the Gulf of Maine. We passed by Isle Au Haut too far offshore for even a glimpse of the faintest outline of the landmark Duck Harbor Mountain.

Too many miles of sea lay between the island and myself. The same miles that I have sometimes regarded as a buffer zone felt like a barricade. I have taken life and living from the sea, and have given the same back, I suppose. The complex and all-consuming ocean feeds man, but also feeds upon men. The flat calm that gently digests my troubles is capable of violent turbulence of enough gluttony to chew up and spit out vessels of the strongest steel, often swallowing men and ships whole. The ocean which gives so much takes back what it needs, commanding respect and getting it from those who have seen and understand the hunger.

EPILOGUE

I lost count long ago of the men I have worked with on the decks of boats. I remember relatively few of their names and faces, and consider fewer still as friends. Although I have lost track of both Charlie (who made a quick and full recovery to the picture of health) and Peter, all five crew members of the *Hannah Boden* described in the chapters of this book are included among the men whom I regard with respect and admiration. I truly appreciate their hard work and dedication to the profession of fishing. I liked the way they treated me as their captain; I think of them as friends.

I had been away from swordfishing for two years in January 1998. Inshore lobster fishing with my own boat suits me, allowing me to catch up on all that I thought I might have been missing in fifteen years of fishing offshore. When I drove from Maine to Gloucester, my intentions were to visit with Bob Brown and retrieve my volumes of personal log books from the wheelhouse of the *Hannah Boden*. Arriving at the dock in Gloucester at 7:45 A.M., I stepped out of my car and into a sunny and crisp winter morning. Filling my lungs with a breath of cold salt air, I thought, God, I miss this, and for a moment entertained the thought of running the *Hannah Boden* again.

The tide was dead low, exposing more of Gloucester than I was accustomed to seeing. It seemed that I would run out of rungs before getting far enough down the ladder to step across to the rail of the boat. Hopping from the rail, I landed on the deck with a thud and quickly made my way through the door and into the warmth of the fo'c'sle, where Bob sat drinking a mug of coffee at the galley table. He appeared to be glad to see me, and stood up, extending his hand for me to shake. Taking his hand, I gave him a peck on the cheek, something that caused his face to flush, which was precisely why I did it. Bob had become a true friend over the years, allowing me glimpses of a real personal charm through the hairline cracks of his hard-assed and professional shell. No longer employed by him, I had become quite fond of Bob, calling on him often for advice and sometimes just to say hi.

We visited across the familiar galley table, talking about boats and fishing. After two cups of coffee and half a dozen sea stories, we climbed the stairs to the bridge, where I found the books filled with notes, lists, and fishing logs from my five years at the helm of the *Hannah Boden*. Five years of my life, so many memories, both good and bad, all reduced to what I could easily carry under one arm. "The boat will be ready to sail tomorrow morning. If you'll agree to take her, I would agree to give you your job back," Bob said, knowing that I would probably refuse his offer, as I had several times in the recent past.

"No, thanks. I'm happy doing my own thing for now." Staring at the notebooks, I added, "Jesus. This is all I have to show for all that work. There's got to be more to life than this."

"What more would you want? You make a good living doing what you love. That's more than most people have."

"Yeah, I guess. But I've been fishing since I got out of school. I think I missed out on a lot by being at sea so much. I just wonder if I'm doing the right thing."

Bob laughed and said, "I'm sixty years old, and I still wonder the same thing. It's human nature to question what you've done with your life."

Bob offered to buy breakfast before I headed back to Maine. I looked at the dock through the back door of the wheelhouse. The tide was now at just the right level to step from behind the house to the top of the dock, but the boat, held off by a "camel," was too far from the wharf. The camel is a large round log that lies horizontally in the water between boat and dock; its purpose is to prevent the boat from chafing or bumping against the cement pier. This particular camel was three times as big around as a telephone pole, leaving a gap that would remain untried by my short legs. "I'm going below and climbing up the ladder."

"Me, too," said Bob, and he was right behind me as I descended the stairs to the lower deck.

I laid the notebooks on the rail to free both hands for the ladder, and as I climbed I yelled to Bob to toss my books up to me. I reached the top of the ladder and turned to see Bob jacking himself up the rungs with one hand, holding my notebooks with the other against his chest. The sixty-year-old came up the ladder with the speed and agility of a young boy. When his right hand grabbed the top rung of the ladder, he stopped. He hesitated for a second, as if suddenly remembering something and thinking. I thought that perhaps he wanted to hand me the books, and I knelt on one knee to reach for them. Bob never looked up. He turned to his right, bent slightly at his waist, released his grip from the ladder, and fell. He fell headfirst for what seemed an eternity. It was not a Hollywood fall. There was no screaming, no windmilling of arms or flailing of legs. It was a silent and motionless fall through stone-cold salt air. He fell, I thought, like a dead man. Both silence and downward motion were broken when Bob's head hit the camel. Never raising his arms to break his fall, he made a one-point landing squarely on his forehead. The sound is what I remember most, and it sickens me still today...a baseball bat striking a melon, then silence.

The rest is a blur. An ambulance, emergency room, tests, hemorrhaging of the brain, swelling, head trauma, and a helicopter ride to Boston. Two weeks later a blood clot and massive heart attack finished what began at the top of the ladder. Bob died. I miss him.

As I said, I lost track of two of the men who fished this trip with me, but the others are good about keeping in touch. Kenny is in Toronto, working at a fiberglass shop. Ringo is fishing aboard a gillnetter out of Gloucester, and Carl is running a stern trawler out of Portland, Maine. As for myself, I am fishing for lobster in the waters surrounding Isle Au Haut. I enjoy being home, but I do miss catching fish and am contemplating buying a larger boat. I often find myself staring to the east, beyond the islands. My thirst for home, seemingly quenched, has been replaced by a slight growling of the stomach. This is the first symptom of sea fever: a passion for bluer waters and bigger fish.

Appendix

SETTLEMENT-10/27

HANNAH BODEN
Captain: Linda Greenlaw
Left 8/30
Returned 9/28

SWORDFISH   Average= $2.61/pound*

RECEIPTS

TOTAL RECEIPTS:	$133,001.40
OVERHEAD	
8% of total receipts:	10,640.11
NET	
Total receipts minus 8%:	$122,361.29

*This trip was a slammer fish-wise, but an average price of $2.61 is dreadfully low. The paychecks were thus disappointing considering the total weight of fish loaded.

BOAT EXPENSES

BAIT	$7,920.00
FUEL	10,389.44
MAIN LINE	1,458.00
LUBE OIL	796.40
GEAR	11,279.40
BRUSHES, FID	21.40
FILTERS	104.95
FILTERS	182.28
ICE	380.00
RADIO BUOY BATTERIES	912.00
FILTERS	240.00
MISC. SUPPLIES	108.95
DISTILLED WATER	10.13
OILER, GREASE	21.98
BRUSHES, ETC.	23.64
CLEANING SUPPLIES	144.54
MAIN LINE	993.68
PARTS RETURNED	(8.05)
PARTS—WATERMAKER	36.75
MISC. SUPPLIES	14.82
MISC. SUPPLIES	37.15
TELEPHONE	157.12
WHARFAGE	2,605.35
DIVER	100.00
TRUCK	100.00
GAS AND TOLLS	58.82
ICE MACHINE	2,000.00
TOTAL BOAT EXPENSES:	$40,088.75

NET, MINUS EXPENSES:	$82,272.54
BOAT SHARE	41,136.27
TOTAL CREW SHARE	41,136.27
CAPTAIN SHARE:	
10% of net minus expenses	8,227.25
CREW SHARE:	
50% of net minus expenses, minus captain's 10%	32,909.02

CREW EXPENSES

FOOD	$3,113.28
TELEPHONE	116.30
TELEPHONE	57.02
TOTAL CREW EXPENSES	$3,286.60

NUMBER OF CREW SHARES	6
CREW EXPENSE PER MAN	$547.77

CREW LIST

LINDA	GROSS	$13,712.09
CARL	GROSS	5,484.84
CHARLIE	GROSS	5,484.84
KENNY	GROSS	5,484.84
PETER	GROSS	5,484.84
RINGO	GROSS	5,484.84

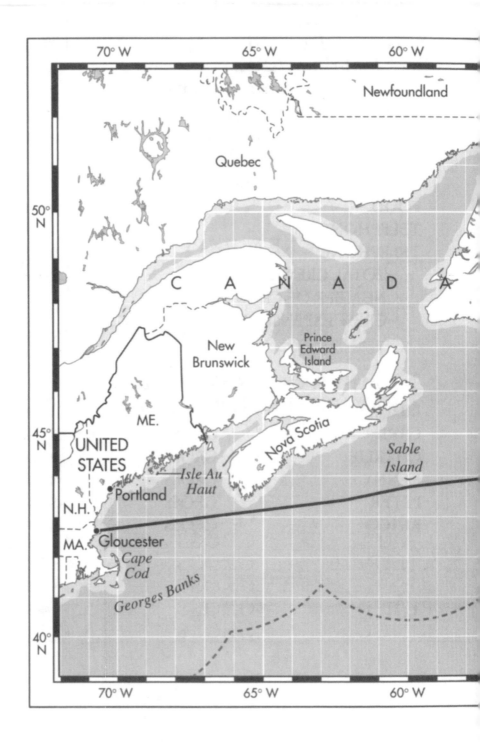

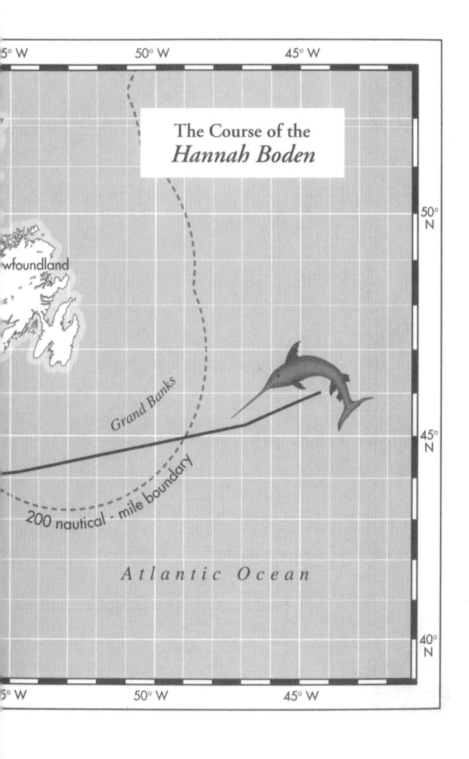

5° W   50° W   45° W

The Course of the
Hannah Boden

50°
N

wfoundland

Grand Banks

45°
N

200 nautical - mile boundary

Atlantic Ocean

40°
N

5° W   50° W   45° W

ACKNOWLEDGMENTS

Thank you, Sebastian Junger, for helping to open the eyes and minds of so many readers. Many thanks to my proofreader and self-proclaimed "number one fan," my mother, Martha Greenlaw. Thanks to my editor, Will Schwalbe, and my agent, Stuart Krichevsky, who have both exhibited amazing patience while working with this first-time author. Thank you, Tom Ring, for supplying the photographs on the back jacket, which I promised to return and probably never will. Thanks to all my friends and family for your interest and moral support.